THE
SUCCESS
FACTOR

THE SUCCESS FACTOR

STORIES FROM SUCCESSFUL ENTREPRENEURS WHO THRIVED AFTER FACING FAILURE

CHERYL POLOTE-WILLIAMSON

purposely
created
PUBLISHING

THE SUCCESS FACTOR

Published by Purposely Created Publishing Group™

Copyright © 2018 Cheryl Polote-Williamson

All rights reserved.

Scriptures marked NIV are taken from the New International Version®. Copyright © 1973, 1978, 1984, 2011 by Biblica, Inc.™. All rights reserved.

Scriptures marked NKJV are taken from the New King James Version®. Copyright © 1982 by Thomas Nelson. All rights reserved.

Printed in the United States of America

ISBN: 978-1-947054-92-9

Special discounts are available on bulk quantity purchases by book clubs, associations and special interest groups. For details email: sales@publishyourgift.com or call (888) 949-6228.

For information logon to:
www.PublishYourGift.com

Table of Contents

Foreword

As of the printing of this book, there are over four billion results when you Google the word "success." It seems to be common knowledge that success has been defined in many ways, from spiritual laws of success to ten steps to success. The amount of literature on success could certainly be perceived as overwhelming and excessive, however, there is clearly a desire that we all have to know, understand, and achieve success. The visionary and authors of this book have opened their hearts and minds to share what has made them successful in various fields and endeavors.

What better time than right now to look at your dreams, goals, and aspirations and juxtapose them with what these authors have shared about their journeys to achievement and positive outcomes? Ideally, you should see the tremendous potential that lies within you to experience the success that you desire. This is not to say that you haven't been successful already, however, I know that if you have tasted the fruits of success in the past, then with great certainty, you want that taste of victory again. You've heard the saying, "Success begets success," so the timing couldn't be better to immerse yourself in stories of success—stories that will add fuel to your rocket to your next-level win.

While each of the stories you read will have the unique lessons and experiences from its respective author, you should comfortably land on your own definition of success. That is really where it begins. I truly believe that happiness is an inside job. Therefore, we have to take personal accountability for what makes us happy and determine how we individually obtain happiness. I often find people seeking success by obtaining some dream, goal, or aspiration. They believe that obtaining that personal outcome will make them happy. I submit to you that you should establish and express your own definition of success. You have a journey that can eventually lead you to your heart's goal and desired outcomes.

If you have started your pursuit of success, then great. You should find this book an inspiration to keep you on track and advance toward your desired outcomes. If you haven't begun, then this is one of many steps you will take to get on the path toward success. This book will enumerate the steps that each author took to experience not only a major success but the valleys and hilltops they journeyed through to ultimately ascend to the pinnacle of their dreams and goals.

As someone who recognizes the importance of leaving a legacy and works daily to establish something of significance to leave to my children and the generations thereafter, I encourage you to embrace and enjoy *Success Factor* as an inspirational read that should energize you on your journey to success.

Russell M. Williamson, Sr.
Bestselling Author
Transformational Leader
Strengths Performance Coach

Awaken Your Inner Hero

BECKY A. DAVIS

*"You did not choose Me, but I chose you and
appointed you that you should go and bear fruit,
and that your fruit should remain, that whatever you ask
the Father in my name He may give you."*
— John 15:16 NKJV

I started my business five years ago. My company was making six figures in the second full year. I closed my first client for $15,000 within three months of launching and my second client for $20,000 two months later. Within two years, I was asked to do a 15-city speaking tour for a multi-million-dollar company. Within three years, I signed a two-year agreement to be the national spokesperson for the Coca-Cola Company's Women's Entrepreneur Initiative. Within that time, I was featured on ABC, TV One, and Fox and in *Black Enterprise, Essence, Huffington Post, Forbes,* and *Rolling Out* magazine, just to name a few. I've spoken on some of the biggest platforms and stages all over the United States. At five years, I signed a new three-year agreement with The Coca-Cola Company to sponsor my bi-monthly luncheons and my entrepreneur webinar series and to not only be a spokesperson, but a speaker, panelist, moderator, or facilitator for any of their thousands of partnership events. My business has grown to mid–six figures.

None of this happened without challenges, struggles, frustration, overwhelm, and fear. With all of this success, I also experienced a lot of failures in the last five years. I launched a product that no one purchased. My first teleconference training had only two people on the call, and one of them was me. I started a training program that no one registered to attend. One person purchased a ticket for my first conference. I gave away 30 free tickets, and only ten people showed up. I've rebranded three times. I changed my title three times. I hired a coach who did not do anything they promised. I partnered with people who did not keep their end of the agreement and left me hanging. I lost money and had to do extra work. I submitted pitch proposals to a hundred companies and received a call from only one.

Success does not happen without failures. Success comes from failures. When you start to see failures as a stepping stone to success and a way to stop, reflect, and reposition, things will begin to shift for you.

I'm excited to share my journey, essential learnings, and my success formula for your journey of entrepreneurship.

When I read John 15:16, I said, "Me? God chose me? That can't be true. Why me? I'm not good enough, smart enough, wealthy enough." Have you ever said these words? I said them to myself every time I was being pushed toward greatness and outside of my comfort zone. It was an internal battle of the mind and spirit. We find it hard to believe John 15:16. After spending time with that scripture, it began to settle inside me. I read it daily until I believed it.

Being a superhero buff, I love Spider-Man, Batman, Wonder Woman, Iron Man; you name it. The superhero and villain stories are centuries old and are still being told today in stories and movies. We love when the hero saves the day. You don't see their power as regular people; it's not until crisis arises that you see the superhero emerge, or as I call it, until they tap into their inner hero. Clark Kent's inner hero is Superman, Peter Parker's inner hero is Spider-Man, Diana Princess's inner hero is Wonder Woman—you get what I'm saying. Their inner hero kicks in when they need to make a difference in someone's life. Who's your inner hero?

I have come to realize that inside of each one of us, there is an inner hero and an inner villain. Your inner hero says that you were chosen and appointed for something great. Unfortunately, the inner hero lies dormant inside a high percentage of people, while the inner villain is alive and well. Success began for me when I awakened my inner hero at different stages in my life.

Our inner hero represents our full potential, our best self, the one designed by God that made us unique, limitless, and the one who needs to be in charge of our life.

Our inner villain fights against our growth and does all it can to rob us of our confidence, trying to prevent us from developing and growing so that we don't live out our purpose.

While working in corporate America, my life was great—at least I thought. Being promoted on average every two and a half years to the next level, I had a successful career by almost anyone's definition. I was successful and being groomed for the top-level management role within the company. When you realize you are good at something and you are working on your gift, you can't help but feel like you've made it. That's what I felt.

It wasn't until I was reading *Keys to Success: The 17 Principles of Personal Achievement* by Napoleon Hill that I realized that maybe I wasn't successful. I picked up the book because I had just been promoted and needed to learn from experts about success. The very first chapter, Develop Definiteness of Purpose, stopped me in my tracks. I began asking myself questions like:

- What is my definite purpose?
- Am I doing the work that I want to do for a lifetime?
- Where am I going?
- Am I limiting myself?

Hill said, "Ninety-eight out of every hundred people never really know their purpose, so they never achieve lasting success." "Whoa! What do you mean?" I said to myself. "I have success!" Then I began to ask myself more questions.

- How am I defining success?
- Is it success or the appearance of success?
- Who do I measure my success against?

These questions led me down a path that took me further into looking at my life with a new set of eyes. When I learned the seventeen principles, I realized that I was so far off from what I thought success was. I could check off only five of the seventeen principles. I realized that I needed to operate at a higher level. I was awakening to something new, and my inner hero was opening her eyes. This journey made me question my role in corporate America. I had always wanted to be a speaker, but this was the first time I thought it was possible. I began my exit strategy from corporate America.

Three years after reading the book, I had fully awakened my inner hero. It was the first of many times that I would need to awaken my inner hero. I realized that real success comes from working in your God-given gift and living out your definite purpose. It's not easy because your inner villain seeks to stop you from your goal.

I've learned that it takes four Cs to awaken your inner hero. You have to tap into these four Cs over and over until it starts to become a habit.

After watching the new Wonder Woman movie, I realized that Wonder Woman used all of these Cs to make a difference in the world, and you can too.

Courage – The ability to act in the presence of fear. It requires courage to become who you "really" are.

I was afraid to leave my consistent paycheck to start my business. It took a near-death experience to show me that tomorrow was not promised. I did not want to leave this world with all my gifts and purpose never being used to their fullest potential. I had to use courage. It took courage for me to give my notice and leave a six-figure job on my way to running an entire brand. It took courage not knowing when I would get my first clients. It took courage to believe that God would never leave the righteous forsaken.

Every day as an entrepreneur takes courage to keep going when you want to quit. It takes courage to ask for the sale. It takes courage to ask for help when you know you need it. It takes courage to keep pushing ahead when you are not making any money, the bills are coming in, and you are figuring out how to live. It's not easy. But let me assure you that you can be successful when it does not look like it and you don't see any signs of it. Courage is not the absence of fear, but the ability to act in the face of fear.

I needed courage when I was asked to be the speaker on a 15-city tour. It scared me silly. What if the audience doesn't think I'm good? What if I'm not that good? I asked myself these questions too many times. I had to tap into my inner hero and fight my inner villain. This is what you must do every time fear arises.

For example, I once created an online program that I was very excited to share. When it launched, no one purchased it. I spent a lot of money on the establishment of the program with videos and marketing. I lost a lot of money, and that made me fearful of launching anything else. I finally realized that my client didn't ask for what I created. I decided to do it because I thought it was good, but my customer didn't. It took me a minute to muster up the courage to jump back in and create again. You will fail in business; you will make some mistakes, because it's all a part of growth. My biggest lesson in that situation was to find out what your customers want before spending a lot of unnecessary money.

You have to push past all your negative thoughts and doubts and convince yourself to move forward. Don't worry about convincing everybody. When others tell you what you can't do, don't focus on proving them wrong. Concentrate on proving yourself right—that you can not only do it, but do it well.

When you are afraid, take action. Sitting and doing nothing keeps you stuck. Do something. Even when you don't know the right thing to do, take action, and the rest will reveal itself along the way.

Fear does two things: it paralyzes and it steals. It will paralyze you from doing anything. It creates procrastination. It steals your dreams, ideas, fear, innovation, and your purpose if you let it. Fear is your inner villain trying to stop you from success. The Joker is always plotting to stop Batman. Guess what? Your inner Joker is doing the same to you.

When you need courage, awaken your inner hero by doing these three things:

1. Pray. It builds your spiritual muscle to fight longer and harder.
2. Read something encouraging or that educates you.
3. Take action. Step into the fear by taking a step that you're afraid of making.

You will learn that you have more courage than you think. Wonder Woman is courageous as a little girl, trying things she is told not to do. She pushes to be a warrior earlier than she is supposed to. She dares to fight the men who attack her island when her mother wants to shelter her. She has the courage to leave a safe island and go into the unknown world to save people. Guess what? You, too, have courage inside of you waiting to be pushed into action. To awaken your inner hero, you need to be courageous.

Commitment – Staying loyal to what you said you were going to do long after the mood you said it in has left you.

It's easy to say what you are going to do when you feel great and you are excited, but it's what happens when you come down from that high that matters.

I was committed to having a successful business by serving and using my purpose-given gifts as the driving force. I've always had financial goals for different stages in my business. There have been days when I did not hit those goals or even come close, and I'd sit and say, "Maybe I was reaching too far." I remember in my first year, I generated no revenue for three months. I was out pushing and promoting, but nothing closed. My commitment started to grow weak. When something like this happens, you begin to question yourself and your skills. The inner villain starts talking, trying to discourage you, making you feel like a failure for not hitting your goals and for not making any money. So you start to alter your commitment. You must pull yourself out of that place.

In the new Wonder Woman movie, she is committed to saving the world and getting to the person who could end the war of all wars. Fear does not stop her even in the midst of battle. It is something bigger at stake that is her driving force. When you get tired or lazy or discouraged and you are losing your commitment, awaken your inner hero and ask yourself:

▸ Who is impacted if I don't keep pushing?
▸ What do they lose if I quit?
▸ What's more important, how I feel right now or the impact I could have on someone in the future?

These questions have a way of getting you back on course and pushing your inner villain out. Stay committed to your journey, and you will see success.

Capabilities – Requires you to rise above your perceived limitations to discover new levels of what you can do.

On my journey as an entrepreneur, I've learned that I'm capable of more than I thought possible.

Technology is not my strength by far, and it was intimidating to me. I didn't want to do social media or email marketing. It was something that my kids did, and I didn't want to be a part of it. My coach said, "If you don't have a social media presence to create social proof, then don't expect growth quickly. Reduce your revenue goals." Well, that was enough to make me do it. Initially, I struggled because I didn't know what I didn't know, which started me on a quest to learn the basics. I began to do research. I took a couple of webinars and attended a teleseminar training on social media and email marketing. It wasn't as hard as I was making it out to be. I got so involved in it; I was teaching my husband, the technology guy, and my kids things about social media.

It's easy to say what you can't do, but what you really mean is that you don't know how to do it. Stop counting yourself out because of what you don't know. Stretch your capabilities. We put more limits on ourselves than on other people. If you don't know how to write a great sales proposal or effectively pitch or name your area of opportunity, here is what you can do to awaken your inner hero and increase your capabilities:

- ▶ Research
- ▶ Get help
- ▶ Try it

These steps have helped me to improve my capabilities. There is more to you than you know, and some will never know because they don't push their limits and increase their capabilities. Every hall of fame athlete, celebrity actress/

actor, Oscar winner, gold medalist, *New York Times* best-seller, and Nobel Peace Prize winner pushed their capabilities to learn and become more.

In the Wonder Woman movie, Diana does not know her full capabilities at first. Her mother even talks about it to the other women after finding out that Diana is secretly being trained by one of the ladies, and she tells the trainer that Diana does not know that she was the chosen one. Her mother doesn't want her to start her battle training as a young girl. Her mother knows her capabilities, but Diana does not know the full extent of what she will be able to do in the future. She knows how to fight, but does not know the inner power that lies inside her until she marches through the battlefield of No-Man's Land to save a besieged European village from German forces. There is a shot fired at her, and she deflects it. Then another shot is fired at her, and she deflects it. It's her facial expression that lets you know she realizes the power of her arm shields. She starts to run, taking all the fire, using her arm shields to dodge and deflect hundreds of bullets so that the other soldiers can start defending the city. She is focused on overtaking the enemy so that the families that have no food can eat. This situation increases her capabilities when she pushes herself. Anytime there is a cause greater than you, you tap into an inner strength that you didn't know existed.

When you are in the middle of achieving success, bullets will be fired at you—bullets that look like defeat, failure, or loss will come at you and dig deep inside. Deflect and dodge them by trying something new to stretch your capabilities.

Confidence – Self-assurance from your appreciation of your abilities, qualities, and character.

Confidence takes time to build, yet with a couple of major moments, it can be crushed. Too often, we allow the world to persuade us to believe that our level of accomplishments is equivalent to who we are as a person. This can shake our confidence.

We all struggle with this C at some point in life and business. It's amazing how people can tell you how great you are and how good you are at what you do, yet somewhere inside you, you don't quite believe it. Your inner villain will do everything possible to reduce your confidence.

People who lack confidence say things like:

"I don't know how to do that."

"No one has ever shown me how to do that."

"I'm not good at that."

The reason I know they say things like this is because I've said all of these. Running a business shook my confidence. It was new territory that was unfamiliar. Every time I got ready to speak, I lacked confidence. When I closed a new client, I struggled with confidence, wondering if I would make an impact on them. When I did training events, I lacked confidence.

I began to pray and study the Bible more. I focused on increasing my confidence in my faith, myself, and others. I started believing what God said about me—that I was more than a conqueror, that I can do all things through Christ, that I am fearfully and wonderfully made by Him. When I chose to believe God and the Bible, I began to feel stronger and more confident. Then I decided to believe in what others said about my gift, and finally, I began to believe in myself and build my confidence. I kept saying to myself over and over, "It's okay to be great."

Identify where you lack confidence and go to work on you. Reading increases competence, and competence increases confidence.

Where has your confidence wavered in business?

Are you around people who reduce your confidence?

At the end of Wonder Woman, she identifies the person whom she thought would help her save the world until he reveals that he had different plans to take over the world. She begins to fight, but does not realize the strength of his powers. After he defeats her moves and pins her down, she realizes that the other people on her team did not give up. Someone she cared about was willing to die, and he had no superpowers. Her confidence grows, and she reveals her "real" power. It doesn't matter anymore that the villain had defeated her before. She has the confidence that she can win, and she does.

Sometimes it takes being pushed by others to build confidence. Confidence is a component of success.

Success for me was awakening my inner hero because I believed John 15:16.

The best advice I can give you for success is to awaken your inner hero. There is more to you. There is more in you. You have more to give. You have more to do. You have more people to touch. The world is waiting on your next big idea. Get crystal clear on your purpose, then awaken your inner hero and fight your inner villain. Don't let your villain win. Remember, ninety-eight out of a hundred people don't experience real success because they don't know their purpose or use it. Don't be in the ninety-eight.

Time to go to work. Which C do you need to strengthen first? _____

Since you know that I love superheroes, I have an inner hero name. I am Becky Davis, but my inner hero is Triple Threat—one for the father, one for the son, and one for the spirit. When you awaken your inner hero, what will your inner hero's name be?

Remember, "it always seems impossible until it's done." — Nelson Mandela.

The Pursuit of Success

SHERRELL VALDEZLOQUI

"But I have raised you up for this very purpose,
that I might show you my power and that my name
might be proclaimed in all the earth."
—Exodus 9:16 NIV

The way we personally define success plays an important role in how we pursue success in our business and personal life. If we are not careful, the way we define success or attempt to pursue it can cause discouragement, depression, and wanting to give up. Have you ever wanted to give up on your business or ministry because you felt like after a certain period of time you should have been further along than where you currently were? What about wanting to give up because you've worked your business for years and still find yourself taking money from your personal finances to maintain its upkeep?

I've experienced all of the above as the publisher of *Promoting Purpose* and *Today's Purpose Woman* magazines. Those experiences definitely didn't match my definition of running a successful business, and it was depressing. It wasn't until one night the Holy Spirit revealed to me the impact a successful business should have on others and how I should pursue success according to the definition He had given me. What the Holy Spirit said to me was simple yet powerful. It is what encourages me to continue to walk with my head held high as a successful business owner. And I believe that once I reveal to you what the Holy Spirit said to me on that night, it will help you focus on your pursuit to having a successful business.

If you ask most magazine publishers what made them start a magazine, they would probably tell you that it was always their dream to start one. If you asked me why I started a magazine, you would hear a totally different story. I'd always dreamed of being a model or a lawyer. And if I couldn't do that, I would have settled for having a small bakery selling cakes, cookies, and other little treats because I enjoy baking and I have a sweet tooth.

None of those things happened. Instead, I raised my right hand and joined the U.S Army. I loved the physical training and the challenges, but most importantly, I enjoyed teamwork. There's nothing like cheering for those who are on the same team as you, knowing that no matter who crossed the finish line, as long as they were your teammate, you all were winners. This is why I feel excited when I see fellow Christians winning; when they win, we all win, and that's a win for the Kingdom.

I served in the army for six years, and within those six years, I became a mother and a wife. After the thought of my husband and I both being deployed at the same time and having to leave our daughters behind crossed our minds, we decided it was best if I got out of the army so at least one of us would be home with our daughters.

I was no longer waking up in the mornings to put on combat boots; instead, my place of duty was home. Being a stay-at-home mom was rough for me. I was bored, and I needed something to do. I was used to making money, and to top it off, I was being flooded with the endless possibilities of starting some sort of business working from home with a nice home office, answering phones with people wanting to order whatever it was I was selling. I didn't know what I was going to sell, but whatever it was, I thought people would be calling me, asking questions, and wanting to buy it.

I didn't know how to start my own home business, so my attention turned to companies that told me that by signing up with them, I would be my own boss and experience financial freedom in no time. This seemed interesting to me. If I signed up, I could work from home, work when I wanted to, and according to the testimonies, be successful in as little as six months. In as little as six months after purchasing the starter kits to three companies, I only sold one item. That was a sign for me to find something else.

About a year later, another idea came to my mind. This idea seemed promising, and it was something I could do on my own. I decided I wanted to start my own greeting card business. I loved writing poems, and I enjoyed encouraging others, so what better way to exercise that than with custom greeting cards. Now this really excited me, and to add to the excitement, as soon as I told a few friends what I was doing, they started ordering cards for birthdays, Mother's Day, and Father's Day. Some people even ordered sympathy cards for those who had lost a love one.

It was nice, but when things began to slow down and I wasn't making any money, I got bored and decided to call it quits. I realized later that I had a hard time staying with something that appeared to not be moving the way I wanted it to move. If it didn't seem like it would bring me success or some sort of financial freedom fast, I moved on to something else. I remembered being a little frustrated and racking my brain to see what else I could possibly do. And then the Holy Spirit said to me, "By the time you turn 26, you'll have your own business." I smiled and repeated to myself what was said, and I hid that prophetic word in my heart.

In the summer of 2010, a little less than two months away from my 26th birthday, I decided to take the girls on vacation to my parents. My husband was deployed to Afghanistan for the second time. It was during this time that I started feeling something I couldn't really explain. Have you ever felt like there was something inside of you that was trying to break free? A feeling that you were meant to do something great but it didn't match what you were currently doing? This is what I started feeling, and the feeling was so overwhelming that I couldn't rest. As I was feeling this, I remember looking at my left arm as though there was a watch on it and saying, "Lord, I'm about to be 26 years old, and I don't see a building for the business you promised me." I remember feeling out of place and crying because at that moment, I thought perhaps God had forgotten about me. Or worse, what if I had been telling myself that I would have my own business by 26 and mistaking it for the voice of God?

As tears began to roll down my face, I remember saying, "Lord, what am I supposed to do? I feel as though I should be doing something great, but I don't see it." I continued on, saying, "Lord, what do you want from me? What is this I'm feeling?" And just as gentle as ever, the Lord told me He wanted me to start a magazine.

This was very uncomfortable for me, and I asked God for confirmation at least four times. He gave it to me. I don't know what frightened me more: the statistics that told me 80% of magazines fail within one to two years of existence while only 20% survive and are successful, or the fear of not knowing anything about starting a magazine.

The Lord provided me with the vision, mission, and title of the publication as well as a content editor, a mentor me, and contributing writers. He showed me how to create the magazine. He told me to name the magazine *Promoting Purpose* and that its purpose was to highlight men, women, and children who were working on His behalf. He wanted the world to see that He still has vessels working despite what is going on in society. The magazine was birthed with no money—just those who God had touched to help me move forward. This was certainly my reality, and it helped me to understand that God's vision comes with His provision.

I must admit, the first magazine seemed pretty easy. I didn't know anything about magazines, so I relied on God to show me everything. I got into trouble when I got the hang of things and got used to the day-to-day operations. Not only was I starting to get used to everything, I began to feel like things were moving a little too slowly for me and that the growth of the magazine needed to speed up. I wanted my inbox full of messages, subscribers, and advertisers. I wanted to hear my phone constantly ringing with publicists inquiring about how to get their clients in the magazine. I wanted that because to me, that would be a sign that the publication was becoming successful.

Every time I look back on my journey, I thank God for His grace, mercy, and patience. I could just imagine God sitting there, watching me, trying to take His vision and run with it as though it was my own. I wanted to run a successful magazine, and to me, an indication of a successful magazine was having subscribers and store placement. Not only would this be evidence to me that the publication was successful, but it would be evidence to the world as well.

While I was working on trying to get subscribers, doors began to open, and I was invited to do several television and radio interviews. The Lord told me when He gave me the title of the magazine that the name itself would attract people, and it did. After being seen on a few local channels, people began to show interest in the magazine. People wanted to subscribe to the magazine, and this motivated and excited me. During this time, it looked like things were moving. I even received an email from a major distributor who said they were interested in placing *Promoting Purpose* magazine in 300 Barnes and Noble locations. They requested copies of the magazine to show a few higher-ups, and within two weeks of sending in copies, I received a contract.

I was excited and couldn't wait to announce that the publication was approved to be in a major bookstore. I looked through the contract and called with a few questions. The responses I received quickly turned my smile into disappointment. Yes, the publication could be on the shelves, but I would have to cover the printing costs. I was a new business, and there was no way I would be able to cover the cost of printing thousands of magazines each month. I felt sick to my stomach and started asking God why He opened this door for me knowing I would be unable to walk through it. Later, I understood that God would never open a door He knows we are not ready to walk through.

I've learned that there's a cost to doing things prematurely. This lesson came while trying to figure out a price for the magazine subscription. I should have done research when deciding what to charge for subscriptions. I wanted to compete against the big boys and thought to myself, "If other publications are charging little or nothing for their subscriptions, why can't I?" I charged too low and forgot to add in tax and shipping. When it was all said and done, my husband had to come out of pocket each month to help me pay the printing cost for the magazine. On top of that, when the magazines were shipped to me, my husband came out of pocket to help me ship the magazine to the subscribers.

This began to take a toll on our finances, and I could see that it was beginning to be a burden on my husband. I tried selling full-page ads in the print magazine, sometimes for as little as $25 just to try and get some sort of money coming into the magazine. That wasn't really successful because not only did I undervalue myself, but the work I had to do to create the ads and put them in the magazine took up a lot of my time. This was truly a disaster for me, and this project was on the verge of being something else at which I would fail.

As soon as the one year was up with the subscribers, I stopped the magazine subscriptions and went to print on demand. Although doing this had lightened the load, it didn't make me happy. Instead of moving forward, I felt like I was going backwards. Depression and discouragement had consumed me. For three years straight around the time of my birthday, I found myself depressed and not wanting to be bothered. I recall the enemy saying to me, "Look at you trying to do this magazine, and yet you're not making any money. Where is the money you need, the nice home, office, full staff, and your dream car?" He continued on, reminding me that I was in my late 20s and didn't have a solid career or sense of direction.

It got so bad that when I went to church. I would hardly get excited whenever the men or women of God would say, "Your blessing is on the way." If they called me up and began to prophesize to me about what God was going to do concerning my business and ministry, I would get a little excited and thank God for the word. But when I got back to my seat, it was like the devil was waiting for me to sit down just to say, "I'll take that, thank you very much." I needed encouragement, and only a few people knew that. To everyone else, I was fine because I was Sherrell, the encourager and publisher of a seemingly popular publication. It's funny because people looked at *Promoting Purpose* as a successful magazine, but I didn't.

In the spring of 2015, my husband was a few months away from completing his one-year tour in South Korea. While my husband was stationed in Korea, the kids and I stayed with my parents, and I continued working on *Promoting Purpose*. Things were beginning to pick up, and people respected my work. I was working on putting together the summer issue when out of nowhere, that same feeling that had come over prior to the birth of *Promoting*

Purpose came back again. It was that feeling that something inside of me was fighting to come out—something that was bigger than me.

I immediately said to the Lord, "Okay, God, what are you trying to get me to birth this time?" He said, "I want you to a start a women's magazine as an extension of *Promoting Purpose*. This magazine is going to be a lifestyle magazine that women from all walks of life can connect with because it will speak to their spirit." I remember telling my mom and one of my friends who is a pastor about it. Both were excited and said to go for it because it was needed.

I stepped out and began the process of creating a second publication. I decided to call it *Promoting Purpose Women*. Starting the magazine was not a problem. I'd had five years of experience with *Promoting Purpose*; I used my successes and failures as a guide while developing the new magazine. *Promoting Purpose Women* was a very popular magazine. We featured actresses, well-known life coaches, inspirational reality TV stars, gospel artists, and so much more. I thought, surely this would be the magazine that would allow me to reach the level of success I wanted.

I received several emails from people who wanted to know if I would consider doing subscriptions because they enjoyed the individual copies they were buying. Finally, I was seeing some sort of progress and gained even more confidence and motivation. One year after releasing *Promoting Purpose Women*, my spirit started feeling uneasy. I had this feeling for one whole week and began seeking God for clarity. God began to reveal to me that the feeling I had was to catch my attention concerning something I had missed with the women's magazine. God is very strategic and takes His provision for His visions very seriously—so seriously that He will turn you around over a title if need be. He said to me, "You didn't wait for me to give you the title of this magazine." "Really?" I thought to myself. "This feeling is over the title of the magazine?" I assumed that since it was an extension of *Promoting Purpose*, I would keep the name and just add women to it.

I took a deep breath after feeling the pressure and said, "Okay, Lord, what is the name of the magazine supposed to be? He said, "*Today's Purpose Woman*." He told me that this title would always keep the magazine relevant, and it would speak to those it is purposed to reach. The title would attract non-believers, and when they opened it up, they would eventually believe. I thought to myself, "Well why did you wait a whole year to tell me this?" His immediate response was, "Because it took you a whole year to seek me on this matter or even sense that I was trying to get your attention." Can you imagine how bad I felt when I got that response? I felt convicted and realized how I was too busy to hear God's voice when I needed to.

Before officially changing the name, I was a little worried. I recall thinking to myself, "Everyone is already used to the other title, and changing it may confuse people." I called my friend who is a pastor and told her what God said to me. She laughed and said, "Well, you better change it." I even ran the new name by my husband, and he said, "Well, that sounds much better." My jaw dropped, and within a day, I announced on social media that *Promoting Purpose Women* magazine was officially being changed to *Today's Purpose Woman*.

After the name change, the mission and vision became even clearer. Even the articles changed. Emails started pouring in as to how the magazine was a blessing because of the stories and features it presented. We were talking to the souls of women from all walks of life. There was evidence of growth in every area of the magazine, yet still a back-and-forth struggle from time to time. I still didn't have the correct definition of having a successful business or what success really looked like. So every time I tried to focus on the spiritual aspect, the flesh and enemy would remind me of how I still didn't have the kind of money I wanted. It was during these times that I would lose focus on the major growth and impact both publications were making.

That is, until I sat down in my room one night and asked the Lord to define what He saw as success and if he saw my business as successful.

He said to me, "Yes, you are successful, because in my eyes, success is not obtaining materialistic things nor is it what's in your bank account. Being successful is simply being able to accomplish and fulfill the mission you or your business was created to do."

That was simple, yet they were the words that changed everything for me. When I changed my focus and placed it on the right area, everything grew, including the finances. I am a successful business owner not because of what's in my bank account, but because my business is accomplishing the mission that it was created to do.

Keys to Remember While Pursuing Success:

Evaluate your definition of success.

Know your business mission.

If your business foundation is spiritual, keep it that way.

Never be too busy to notice signs of God trying to speak.

Forgive and move on.

Know your value.

Surrendering to the Spiritual "Style" of Success

LEAH FRAZIER

"Do the thing, and you shall have the power."
—Ralph Waldo Emerson, Essay on Compensation

I was happy, excelling, and feeling fulfilled. At the age of 25, I was a promising young associate at a mid-sized law firm with plans to make it to the top. Not one person or one thing could stop me. Dreams of one day being a judge filled my thoughts, and I buried myself with case after case, slowly ascending the mountain of success.

Innately, I'm a planner. Every minute movement I made, whether personal or professional, was strategically thought through. In my analytical mind, there was no room for risk or error. The life I was building was setting me up for comfort, for the family I desired, and for financial prosperity. At 25, I had it all. Until...

I had a dream, and not in the prophetic Dr. Martin Luther King Jr. type of way. It was a dream about clothing and shopping with women. Go figure. One of my favorite pastimes and often-wasteful ways of spending my hard-earned money had crept its way into my dreams. I was the labeled fashionista of the office and the courtroom, so it wasn't completely far-fetched.

I would arise every morning and fall asleep every night for the next several weeks having the same dream. At this point, I attributed the dream to my closet addiction to reality TV – specifically all things related to fashion and celebrity stylist Rachel Zoe on the Bravo Channel.

Day in and day out, the dream kept reoccurring. Finally, I told God, "Okay. If this is you talking to me, then tell me why am I having this dream? Am I supposed to actually do this? How? Where do I start?" After a week of research and planning, I said, "Yes God, I'll do this," and it was a done deal.

On a secular level, my "yes" did not make sense. An attorney turned fashion expert? Try explaining that one! On a spiritual level, it was the perfect depiction of who God really is.

A simple "yes" has changed the lives of countless women through fashion and style. A simple "yes" has broadened my platform to journalism, with works published by CBS, *Examiner*, *Belong Magazine*, other top-tiered outlets, and my own blossoming digital magazine, *Inspire N Style*. A simple "yes" has led to interviews with globally renowned designers, coverage at New York Fashion Week, invitations to Paris Fashion Week, event and brand partnerships with Neiman Marcus, Belk, Cantu Beauty, and Marshall's—the list is endless.

A simple "yes" has led to a life in media, being coined as the expert in fashion and style on Fox News, Good Morning Texas, NBC, CW, and many more. A simple "yes" has led to the creation of four businesses, including my most recent venture, Think Three Media. A simple "yes" allowed me to walk away from law, to truly live in my purpose, and to live a life that I had never imagined.

A simple "yes" changed it all—but of course, not without challenges, pitfalls, and setbacks. As Frederick Douglass once said, "If there is no struggle, there is no progress." And this was where true growth and true success blossomed—within the struggle.

The Climb: Get Ready and Just Do It

The road from the courtroom to the runway was paved in anything but gold—and it surely wasn't glamorous. I humorously compare the road to one filled with cobblestones, potholes, and every type of hazard you can imagine. Just close your eyes and envision an obstacle course with winds, curves, and extremities for an accurate depiction. I wasn't aware of the trials ahead, but despite opposition, I was determined to succeed.

In the beginning of my purpose discovery, things were relatively easy. I would work tirelessly in the law office all day and then morph into a taller, curvier version of Naomi Campbell by night. It was as if all the doors were opening magically and I was a magnet attracting opportunity after opportunity. I made my first television appearance within two months of starting my business and soon escalated to one of the area's top fashion reporters in less than a year of contracting for *The Examiner.*

Lesson Number One: God Will Qualify You

It was at this point that I learned my first valuable lesson, and that was God will qualify you at whatever level you're at and wherever you are. While this phrase is partially synonymous to "your gifts will make room for you," it actually goes a step further.

How often have you talked yourself out of an opportunity or your passion because you were not formally trained in that area? Or maybe you thought people would think you were crazy for taking a leap into a completely different industry? Or maybe you have convinced yourself that you don't have enough resources. Does any of this sound familiar?

Once I accepted God's call, I slowly realized that this simple acceptance was the first step. Remember, many are called, but few are chosen. As I began stepping into a new and unfamiliar territory of fulfilling my purpose, the resources began to appear. The network that was non-existent began to grow. Doors that I never knew existed began to open. Mentors who could educate me within the industry surfaced.

It was at this point that I adopted one of my many mantras, and that was "the fulfillment of purpose is a 'one-foot-in-front-of-the-other type of journey.'" You will never have it all together, but you have to trust that God (not the world) will qualify you in your purpose along the way. God uses ordinary people to do extraordinary things. He's just looking for that "one foot in front of the other" mentality within the journey. Stop worrying about the "what ifs" and just do. You'll realize that taking the small steps of action allows God to fill in the missing pieces in a supernatural way.

The Magic of Mindset

During my fifth year of juggling a career as a full-time attorney with after-hours and weekends of personal styling and fashion blogging, I began to grow weary. It was difficult to keep up the façade of attorney by day and fashionista by night when I wanted to pursue fashion full-time. I was frustrated. While I was seeing progress over the years doing both, my double life was taking its toll. I began to suffer physically, mentally, and emotionally.

I met my business coach at the height of my frustration. Her ways of thinking, business acumen, and strategies really piqued my interest. After attending one of her events followed by a multi-day conference, I explored the possibilities of one-on-one business coaching. The only problem was the extremely hefty price tag. Sticker shock was definitely an understatement at the time.

During the time of our meeting, I was saving for my first home. I had just completed pre-qualification for a mortgage, and as in-house counsel for a major bank, the perks for the mortgage were unmatched. You couldn't get this great of a deal if you tried. When the offer was presented for a year-long coaching session, I only had less than 24 hours to make a decision and to sign the contract. It was do or die. While I knew I was exhausted and that this coaching program could be the solution to my problems, I couldn't get past the price. Ironically, the price for the program was almost (to the penny) the price I had saved as a down payment for my first home.

I cried and cried until I fell asleep. Financially, I had always been secure. Thoughts of how hard I worked to save and to earn the money tormented me. I prayed to God to give me the wisdom for the right decision, but he responded, "You already know what to do." In my mind, I was hoping that it wasn't to sign away everything I had worked for, but that was apparently the price I had to pay. I woke up the next morning with the tear-stained contract stuck to my face. I filled it out diligently, held my head high, and turned it in to the coach. I was desperate. I needed answers for my business, and I needed them then, before I hit complete burnout.

After I turned in the contract, I only had a few business days to complete the financial transaction. The very next day, I walked into my bank, held my head high, and requested the sum in a cashier's check. The teller looked at me, gave me a big smile and said, "Congratulations on your new home!" My heart sank. I swallowed my tears and said, "Thank you, but I'm not buying a home." I grabbed my check and cried all the way to my business coach's bank. In my limited mindset, everything I had worked for was now gone. My security—gone.

Lesson Number Two: For Success, You Must Invest

At this point, I didn't realize that God was teaching me a multitude of lifelong lessons. From leaning on Him as my security instead of money to the ultimate gut check of "how bad do you really want it," this point in my journey was the catalyst for my destiny.

Think about it: if everyone could reap the benefits of destiny without any contribution, then we'd all be prosperous and living our lives with purpose because we could reap from God without any investment from our end. The pain of growth and sacrifice would not be required.

On my journey, my investment was the one thing I wanted the most—my first home. Later on, my path would require other personal luxuries that I would soon have to release. As I weighed my options, one end of the scale was a life of security, comfort, and the ordinary, but at least everything was mapped out and perfectly planned. On the other end of the scale was a life of uncertainty, the unknown, and the immersion of complete and total faith in God, but also a life of expectation and possibly the key to extraordinary. In weighing these, which one would you choose? Are you at this crossroads currently? What is He asking you to invest into your destiny?

Obviously, I chose the unknown. If God had brought me this far, I knew He wouldn't hang me out to dry. Fast forward, I paid for the year-long coaching program, and within 30 days, my business coach taught me how to make my money back. I signed several contracts that totaled the amount of my investment almost immediately upon paying for her services.

I truly believe that God continually tests us—our strength, our mindset, and our spiritual willpower. This test of my investment, although on the surface monetary, was more so about my faith and trust in Him rather than the actual dollars. Was I willing to risk it all on the notion that He would provide? Was I willing to invest everything I had worked so hard for on the notion that this was His plan for my life?

You bet, and I haven't looked back since. Post climbing that hurdle, taking risks has become easier and critically essential to my success, because I know that if it's in alignment with my purpose, God will carry me through. In the words of LeeAnne Womack, "Never settle for the path of least resistance."

You Have Absolutely Nothing to Lose

Once I worked past the pain that my dream home was on pause, I began to focus on my destiny. I worked around the clock to build my businesses and my expertise up to a level that was competitive and highly marketable. Less than a year of following the business plan my coach developed, I was able to transition to a full-time fashion entrepreneur.

The journey was exhilarating, and the freedom was incomparable to anything I could have imagined. However, I wasn't prepared for the level of noise within the marketplace. Frankly, it was deafening. Everywhere I looked, there were other entrepreneurs with similar businesses, comparable strategies, and stellar ideas. And in the world of social media and marketing, it appeared as though my colleagues were progressing at speeds 100 times faster than I was. I began to grow anxious. Was I not doing enough? Was I not working hard enough? Was I simply not enough?

Lesson Number Three: Stand Firm In Your Gift

Over time, I learned several important lessons in the case of building a business in a competitive and noisy marketplace, the first being that your gift is your gift, uniquely embedded within you. There is no one on this Earth who can do what you do and in the manner that you can do it. Once you realize that, the noise becomes silent, your focus narrows, and your sense of worth increases.

In all honesty, I wasn't sure that I had a gift. When it came to my role as a fashion reporter, I thought that I was just another crab in the bucket fighting my way to the top. This was my outlook until I realized that at most of my interviews, the subject would cry, revealing their innermost thoughts, or the subject would divulge their deepest and darkest secrets that they wouldn't dare tell another journalist.

I would often question, "Why does this keep happening? Why do they trust me? Why are you telling me this?" And they would all say the same thing, "There's just something about you." Or "I just feel so comfortable around you." It was in these moments that I knew I had a gift—a gift of human connection, and not just in the reporting sense, but across all my platforms. And it was within this connection that my most emotionally riveting pieces were birthed and my uniqueness within the marketplace was solidified. In a room full of journalists scrambling for the attention of one individual, I always seemed to get the raw scoop.

Lesson Number Four: Create Opportunity, Don't Wait for Opportunity

Once I unapologetically proclaimed my gift, I took it and ran. I knew what I brought to the table. When God would download the craziest of ideas and business ventures into my head, I went for them, knowing that I had something that the world needed. My attitude then became, "If not now, when?" or "What do I have to lose?"

Standing tall within my gift, I began to flip the script. I became an opportunity-creating, brand-pitching machine. From speaking opportunities to strategic partnerships, I was so confident in who I was and what God had downloaded within me that I was virtually unstoppable. This can be you.

What ideas (no matter how crazy) has God instructed you to move on? What opportunities are you waiting on for your career? Can you make the first move yourself?

Often, we know our gifts and think that because we are talented or because we have had success, that opportunities will gravitate toward us and our work is done. This is only partially true. The real success is in the moments where you know your gift, and instead of waiting for opportunities to arise, you create them yourself. Take charge of your destiny.

Now, in all honesty, I'm known for dreaming up some pretty insane ideas for my brand, and I have encountered hundreds of nos during this process, but the sweet yeses that came through when I took charge of my destiny and pitched myself for an opportunity made the entire process worth it. This one lesson alone made such an impact on my business and brand that I make it a part of my daily business activities to map out my own opportunities for ascension. It's just that important.

*

From steady "one foot in front of the other" action to investments to spiritual confidence, these are the lessons that have helped me on the journey to success. While lessons in business can be painful and never-ending, each one consistently empowers growth, strength, and undoubtedly more faith in and focus on God.

On my journey, I had to realize who and where my security came from. I had to stop worrying about the resources, finances, and networks and take things one day at a time, knowing that God had already done the hard work for me. Instead of joining the crowd of people who never jump because they feel as though they're not prepared enough, I jumped knowing that God would prepare me along the way—and He hasn't failed since.

Once I jumped, I had to learn the process of risk and investment. Separating the secular mindset from the spiritual mindset is daunting. In my case, minimizing my lifestyle and letting go of security in the full power of surrender to Him is what led God to take control and illuminate the path to my destiny.

After the path was illuminated, I realized that there were many travelers on my road. However, once I had complete and total confidence in my gift, I knew that I could be unstoppable. I created more and more opportunities for myself, knowing that I carried something so precious and so unique that it was unmatched. And with that knowledge, the bounds were released from my journey and my businesses were no longer in a box. I went from having one business to owning four, because why not?

Takeaways

1. Get comfortable with letting God be the qualifier and provider for all the things that you feel that you lack. All that He is asking for are small steps or for a "one foot in front of the other" mindset and action process, and He will be working to provide the rest. What small steps and actions can you take every day toward your destiny and purpose?

2. What do you need to invest to take your brand or business to the next level? What are the things that the secular world is telling you are necessary for living, but in reality, you can do without? Could this sacrifice or investment boost your business? Truly evaluate your lifestyle. How bad do you want it? Make as large a deposit as you can into your destiny and watch the favor as God returns the blessing.

3. Truly evaluate your gift and confidently know that this is your unique DNA from God. No one can do what you can do. Stand firm in this belief. Once you have identified what your offering is, get ready to present it to the world. Make it a part of your everyday business strategy to identify ways in which you can create your own opportunities for yourself in alignment with your gift. Whether that is contacting partners for strategic business ventures, pitching for speaking opportunities, or developing innovative products, take the time out daily to put your stamp on the marketplace.

One Day I Will Be Where I Have Always Wanted to Be

COURTNEY WILLIAMSON

"Any life is made up of a single moment, the moment in which a man finds out, once and for all, who he really is."

—Jorge Luis Borges

I would like to think that this single moment of which Borges speaks came to me when I was seven years old. A child goes to the doctor from the time that they are born to the time they become a legal adult and so on. As I grew up going to various appointments, also known as yearly check-ups, I began to develop quite the interest in the doctor I would go to see. She was much like a hero to me. What really grabbed my attention was that I would see this white-coat-wearing woman once or twice or year, but she cared for me as if she knew me thoroughly and loved me. To a seven-year-old Courtney, this was amazing. With that amazement came questions. I asked my parents what kind of doctor the woman was, and when they told me she was known as a pediatrician, I knew I wanted to be one. I knew I had to be one. Most kids bounce around when talking about what they want to be when they grow up, but something in my heart was set firm on being a pediatrician. Such a feeling could only be from the Lord himself, and I have never wavered from that desire to be a pediatrician.

I am a firm believer that one can achieve the life they desire by experiencing multiple wins along with multiple losses. Reaching one's desired goals has never proven to be a fairy tale, and I think anyone would agree, no matter how big or small their goals are. Well, for me, the non-fairy tale parts of my story began at an early age.

I was at the beginning of third grade when I moved back to Texas, and I was going to no longer be attending the school I had previously attended when I left Texas. Therefore, I was the cliché movie child who shows up to a new school in the middle of the year. I had a few observations when I first arrived at the school, but my first was that there were very few—if any—people who looked like me, and by that I mean that the diversity rate was at an all-time low. I had been in similar environments before, but never had I experienced mistreatment because of my skin color. I had a teacher who did not want me to succeed, and she did her best to try to make this so.

One thing I can say about my younger self is that I was what some people consider a "nerd." I loved doing homework, and I loved going to school every day to learn. My favorite thing to do was read. I was learning to play chess and actually starting to get pretty good at it. Because of these interests, I picked up habits, such as never turning in my work late and always being prepared for a lesson.

Well, many times, this teacher tried to, for lack of a better word, "play me" and tell me I had missing work or that I did not complete an assignment. So, like any other child, I complained to my mother about this treatment I was receiving and these false accusations that were being brought against me. In addition to the false accusations, one day I received a bad grade, and if you know me, you know that, although it is not good that I do, I can let a bad grade ruin my day, and I will just feel really torn up about it. After I received the bad grade, my teacher then did a demonstration on the board to show how our grades would average out, and oh, it was just so ironic how the number she used included my bad grade and the other grades I had received. In that moment, I knew it was not a coincidence, but the teacher attempting to take a blow at my confidence in school and to put me down in general. I was so sad after that experience because I could not believe that an adult woman would treat me as if I were any different from any of her other students. Although it may not seem like a big deal to me now, experiences like that can pour negative energy into a child and lead them to believe that they are less than they are.

In addition to the unfortunate experiences with my teacher, the school also had an accelerated learning program known as LEAP. Every day, I would hear about the LEAP kids and what they were learning. When I heard these things about LEAP, I knew I had to be a part of the program because at the time, my thirst for learning was unquenchable. Of course, entering the program required my teacher's recommendation. How unfortunate, if I do say so myself. My mother spoke to my teacher, who said it was too late for me to enter the program, but I think everyone had their disbeliefs about that statement. My mother has always wanted the best for me, and after she spoke with my teacher, I enrolled in the LEAP program and stayed in it for the remainder of my time in elementary school.

Although LEAP was a part of my early life, it instilled the values of loving challenges and finding solutions, which would become integral parts of my future goal of becoming a pediatrician. Now looking back at this experience, I can tell that I learned a lot from LEAP, and it shaped me to love to prove people wrong. To think that I could make someone change their way of thinking by breaking out of their stereotype or misconceptions because of the way I appear makes me smile and fuels me daily to make decisions that the Lord and I would be proud of. Do not let early life experiences reshape the future you see for yourself. Learn from the trials and prosper from them. Had I let the teacher's mistreatment and disbelief affect me in a negative way, I probably would have strayed from the pediatric career path.

After my elementary school experiences, I was beyond ready for a change. One day, I went to my church's additional location, and there was a booth set up for a private Christian school. I would be lying if I said the Lord did not speak to me in that moment and tell me to approach the table. I went to the table and spoke about the school to the representatives. Safe to say, I fell in love instantly. I created a slide presentation not only to show my parents the reasons I should attend the school, but also the reasons the school would be worth the money. I have now been at said school for six years and will graduate in May 2018.

I started at Faith in sixth grade, and it was truly a different experience for me. The standards were much higher, the students were much wealthier, and the Lord was more prevalent here than at any of my other schools. The Lord told me to go to that representative booth for a reason, and I knew it in my heart. At the school, we have chapel every Thursday, where we can come together, worship, and receive a message. At my very first chapel at Faith, I received Christ. My life was truly changed. I found myself craving worship. I wanted to know more about God. I now had something in which to put my faith and hope. Young me had a lot of dreams, and although I had support from my parents, they are only humans. Knowing that I was the daughter of the God who can move mountains, create the world, and love us despite our flaws was what I needed in life. With my new belief in the Lord, my hopes and dreams skyrocketed because I believed that with the Lord, all things were going to be possible. No dream felt too big, and no dream felt too small.

During my time in junior high, there were a lot of challenges I faced that could throw anyone off their path. I saw friends and family stray away from who I had always known them to be, and it hurt me. Seeing people whom I loved so dearly leave the path that I thought they would always be on made me wonder if I could achieve all that I had planned for myself. When doubts began to form, I could have either shut them down or I could have let them fester. Of course, I let them fester. The end of my doubts not only came from God, but also from my parents. Throughout my years in junior high, my parents purchased items that not only encouraged my dream, but also instilled in me a new belief in myself that I could, in fact, do it. They purchased doctor's kits complete with a stethoscope, reflex hammer, and so much more. Not only did I receive a doctor's kit, but I also received a doctor's coat with the name Dr. Williamson stitched on it and a medical dictionary. For some reason, seeing those items around me confirmed in my mind that I wanted this to be my future. Even when a brother and sister in Christ are falling off the path, help them, but don't allow them to take someone else off the path with them.

High school kicked my dreams into the fast lane. Suddenly, they weren't dreams anymore. They were events to prepare for. Ninth grade became a preparatory year for what was to come. Tenth grade became a year to gear up for what was to come. Eleventh grade became the year to set the foundation and see if I even had the ability to achieve everything I wanted. Twelfth grade came much like a slap to the face, but it is the year to see if I will thrive and keep walking on the path to who I want to become.

During my freshman year, I focused on starting activities for my résumé. Looking back, I am glad none of my activities were résumé driven. They were activities in which I wanted to take part. Most of the activities in which I was involved included helping children, and I thrived there. These volunteer opportunities did not just serve as something nice to put on a piece of paper that I would later submit, but they served as surefire confirmations that I wanted to work in pediatrics. Over the course of the year, I realized I had a true passion in my heart for the development and care of children. They are a precious gift with which God has blessed this Earth, and it is mankind's job to make sure those children grow up the way they should.

Tenth grade is when I began to buckle down because I realized the level of academic knowledge and discipline I was going to need if I planned to go to college, then medical school, and on to become a doctor. That year, I worked my tail off. I continued my summer job into the school year and tried to control all aspects of my life, but there is only one person who has control, and that is God. Over the course of the year, I experienced a lot of curve balls that I thought were going to have me cut my dreams short. I began to have feelings of "If I can't balance it all now, how I am going to balance it all later?" But that was the thing; I was trying to balance it all. Just me. I never stopped to put my hope and faith in God that year. It is so easy to struggle once departing from God. If life ever seems like it is falling apart before one's eyes, look to God. He sees us struggling, and he wants to put us back together. There is no number of mistakes that one can make that is too far out of God's reach.

The summer before my junior year, I was able to travel across Europe for two weeks with my classmates. This trip showed me that I wanted to travel and help people around the world. Europe served as a confirmation of my desire to adopt children when I was old enough. I have known that for some time, but had doubts. Even some of my distant family members questioned that dream, but my travels helped me realize that children everywhere needed to be cared for.

Now eleventh grade was the true test. ACT. Résumé. College. Everything was becoming imminent before my eyes. The ACT was my biggest concern. I thought it was going to make or break my college applications. And it's true. I couldn't apply to Harvard with a 21 composite score, and I couldn't go to Brown with a 14 composite score. The thought of taking a test on a Saturday morning that would ultimately determine my path for the next four years after graduation instilled fear within me, but I prayed. A lot. Soon a sense of calm came over me, and on a Saturday in October, I walked into my local high school with no test prep and five hours of sleep and took the ACT. About a month later, I received my scores from that day, and I was more than pleased. With that knocked out, I began to consider where I wanted to go.

During this time, advertisements from colleges would fill my mailbox. I received mail from over 100 colleges, including all the Ivy League schools. Receiving that mail didn't reassure me of my intelligence level, because I was sure a lot of people received it, but it reassured me of my dream. It helped me realize that the world needed quality doctors and that there were universities that were looking to put them through their programs.

The end of my junior year was a series of great events that showed me that I was on the right path. I was a part of a team that won the Women's Soccer State Championship for our school, I went to my first prom, and things seemed to be falling together. The hugest confirmation arrived in January of 2016, but I did not realize it until my junior year. My niece Leah was born in January of 2016, and I did not realize until one random day of babysitting her that she was my human confirmation that I wanted to be a pediatrician. I want the best for her, and I want her to experience all of life's greatest joys. That is my wish not only for Leah, but all children; they are the future.

By the end of my junior year, I had an idea of the colleges I wanted to apply to. I wanted to apply to the University of Texas at Austin, Rice University, Brown University, Case Western University, and Texas Christian University. It was scary to think that I did not have only one absolute yes but multiple yesses. How does one decide their future when it is not clear to them? I keep waiting for a sign from God in favor of a specific college, but it has yet to be revealed to me. During the summer before my senior year, everything somehow became more real than it already had been. I saw my cousin graduate that summer, and suddenly the feeling that I would soon experience the same thing overwhelmed me but also excited me. That summer, I began working and am still working well into my senior year. My most exciting event over summer was starting my own blog. On the blog, I talk about my journey and future, and it is a wonderful way for me to see how I far I have come and how far I will go. When the school year started, I wanted to give myself the ultimate challenge. I have no idea why, but I am in Honors Spanish, four AP classes, Honors Philosophy, and dual-credit English. Life is definitely no walk in the park, but I feel ready to be challenged because that will soon be my life in college and medical school, so why not prepare now?

It is now the beginning of my senior year, and I no longer have five colleges on my list, but eleven: University of Texas at Austin, Rice University, Brown University, Case Western University, Texas Christian University, St. John's University, Tulane University, University of Mary-Hardin Baylor, University of Dallas, Loyola Marymount University, and West Point. How will I choose from these? I have no idea, but I do know that surrounded by my family, friends, and God, I will make the right decision, and I have never been more excited. I have already received one acceptance to University of Mary-Hardin Baylor, and I am hoping for many more.

Life has been a whirlwind of action, adventure, and trials, but I have held on to my dream since I was seven years old. Now I am seventeen. My dreams are slowly becoming imminent realities, and I know that through this whole process, God will have my back.

Are You Leaving Money on the Table?

PEARL CHIARENZA

"Pretend that every single person you meet has a sign around his or her neck that says, 'Make me feel important.' Not only will you succeed in sales, you will succeed in life."

—Mary Kay Ash

My company is called Bodyworks Health & Wellness Center. I started my business after losing 57 pounds with our program. Before that, I was a mortgage loan originator. With our move to Florida, I found that the mortgage business was going to be much harder than expected. That was mostly due to the economy. My children were not happy with our neighborhood, as we went from over ten boys in our neighborhood to three, including my two, and after having a hysterectomy in my late 30s, I started to struggle with weight. I would have never thought my weight loss would allow me to bring income to my family.

I often get asked about lessons or advice I have learned over the years of being a business owner. I have learned to stick to the integrity of treating others the way I would like to be treated and to rely on God and my coach to guide me through decisions or challenges I may have. I would encourage you to reach out to others to learn from their experiences and become involved in your community by giving back through your company. Through my business, I sponsor a woman who has suffered from domestic violence, gifting her with our program for three months. With my community involvement, I have become very resourceful. It is not uncommon for me to receive calls from others who are referred to me because they hear I may know someone who can help them. I am proud of the fact that no matter what, with God's guidance, I will be on the path He has for me with my business and life goals.

I recently sponsored a retreat, and one of the speakers challenged us to write a letter to our younger self. This was not an easy task, but I embraced it for my personal and business goals. If you have never done this, I challenge you to try it, as it is very therapeutic. Looking back, I realized one thing I would have told myself is that while having a large heart for giving is a great attribute, not everyone I partner with will have the same goal. So ensuring that I am aligning with likeminded people is important to accomplishing a win-when working with others. Now, when I work with strategic partners, we write our expectations, revisit them as we work through the process, and evaluate if the agreement is working and in alignment with our vision. Doing this has brought amazing outcomes, such as working with personal trainers, offering cooking classes, and starting a women's empowerment program.

My younger self also needed to be sure to find an expert branding company early as part of the process of starting my business. If you do not incorporate this, you may realize like I did that not doing this earlier in my business did not enable me to get my message out clearly. When defining your message, I encourage you to find what sets you apart from your competition. For me, it is my compassion for my clients. The coach I trained with treated clients like they were failures, did not get to know what was causing the clients' challenges, and failed to thank them for their business. I knew that was not how I wanted to run my business, and I work hard at making sure each client feels special. Our clients will tell you that I never give up on them while I work to empower their lifelong success. They know that I care about them and understand where they have been and where they are going. I do all that I can to ensure that they leave feeling empowered. Our mission is based on our compassion for our clients.

Before opening my health clinic, I had been a health coach for another weight loss clinic that offered a program based on a specific product. The company agreed to let me open my own clinic in two different locations. In preparing to leave the company, I knew as a 1099 employee that I should be able to take my clients with me. In addition, the owner of the clinic had always said that we could take our clients with us if we opened our own clinic. What she did not expect was for me to be the first to achieve the goal of building my clientele and opening a clinic. You see, I was a large part of the business that was coming in the door, so when it came down to it, she realized the loss of business and the challenges it would bring to her clinic. On my last day at the clinic, imagine my surprise when the corporation sent a District Manager in to let me know they were not going to allow me to take my clients. They informed me that if any of them came to my office and they found out, the company was not going to ship me product, and essentially, I would not have my company.

I am sure you are thinking, "Well they cannot tell you that legally! You are like a hairdresser. You can take your clients with you if you want." You would be correct. The challenge was, I only had their products, and if I did not find a way to work it out, I would have had no company, and my family would have struggled financially. I took a deep breath, shared with them that our agreement was not set up that way in the beginning, and then offered a solution. I agreed under the condition that a select group of clients I worked with would need to go with me and that if there was a client who adamantly did not want to stay with the owner of the clinic I was leaving, they would be allowed to come with me. Listen, I knew that some of those I did not have on my list would not stand for that and would still find me to work with me at my clinic, and that is exactly what happened. Looking back, I am proud of myself for sticking to my values, as it is part of my success. One additional lesson from this experience was to incorporate contracts with my coaches I hire as to avoid misunderstanding of expectations.

I knew going into opening my business that the challenges would not stop with that first obstacle. The product I was using at my weight loss clinic was not part of the franchise of the company with which I opened my clinic. Instead, I was a customer. The problem I encountered was that they could choose not to ship me products if I wanted to offer other products or services that went against what they wanted us to carry, causing me to essentially not have additional revenue for my company. So during the next three years, I investigated and watched for a product that could provide my clients the same result. If I changed the product I offered, I needed to ensure that my clients would get the same results as the current product we offered. I was so happy to find that product almost three years ago. The funny part is that the person who had the product was the same District Manager whom they had sent to keep me from taking clients. She, too, did not like the path on which they were going and how they treated their clinics and decided to open her own company by finding manufacturers that offered like products. The bonus was that I could offer the same results at a lesser cost to my clients.

Everything was going great, and as my clients were succeeding on their journeys, they were referring their friends and family. Sounds good, right? Well, yes, until you start getting those referrals who love you but do not want to purchase the products. I found myself turning those clients away, because if they were not going to use the products, how could I help them effectively? I attended an event called Align with Kimberly Pitts of UImpact in Plano, TX, and the ladies at the event opened my eyes! We spent time brainstorming on our companies and the services we offered and identifying additional services and income we could incorporate. This process and the feedback from the ladies in attendance helped me see that my clients were not coming to me for the products! They needed the products to help them on their journey, however, it was my coaching that was a big part of their success. So if you are offering a product and feel stuck in expanding, look at other areas of service you provide and tailor that service to become an income earner. That's what I did, first by looking over the notes of those referrals that had objections to the products and wanted coaching. I made a list of services I could provide them, and implemented new programs. I kicked myself for missing out on additional revenue over the years. We have rolled out three packages that are a big success. Don't get frustrated if you, too, go through the process and the light bulb of missed income pops up, because as I tell my clients, "Life is not a remote. I cannot rewind, so move forward and let God guide you."

I realized that I needed to find a way to work at a higher level because I was missing the opportunity for additional income. I had to sit back and ask myself why. I began a series of empowerment workshops structured with two brunches and one weekend PJ Retreat every year. We bring female speakers who are entrepreneurs or homemakers or have a corporate career to share how they have learned to put themselves first to succeed in their goals. I think part of missing the opportunity comes from staying in a rut of working *in* my business instead of *on* my business. I would consider getting a business coach, as reaching out to one myself helped me start what I call my business homework.

So what does your business homework look like? First, schedule "business homework" on your appointment scheduler where you are dedicating about three to four hours allowing for activities, including social media posting, calls to clients (old and potential), and reviewing programs you are offering. Next, schedule two days each week for one-to-one meetings with potential referral partners or visiting a business you would like to partner with and dropping off a unique basket that sets you apart (our basket is full of protein bars). Lastly, find creative ways to have referral partners bring their clients to your office. At our clinic, we offer a Healthy Happy Hour every week, inviting our referral partners to bring their clients and provide them the opportunity to share their business. You will be amazed at the income you can bring in from incorporating business homework. I have found that when I make calls to clients, my bottom line for the month increases significantly.

This year, I found myself doing another first, and that was creating a vision board. Interestingly, I had heard so much about them, but never made one myself. Yes, I had business goals and had written them down, however, putting together the pieces of the goal into pictures on a board that I can see every day is very motivating. My first vision board includes both business and personal goals. It is a good idea to also have smaller boards to break your bigger goals down into quarterly visions. This enables you to see your vision come alive monthly, quarterly, and yearly. I have gotten to a point where if something or someone presents me with an opportunity, I review my board and ask myself where the opportunity falls in my vision. If it does not fit in your vision, it is okay to say, "Thanks, but no thanks."

I used to think that my conversations with God should be more focused on my family than on my business. You see, I grew up not having conversations with God openly because we were not taught how to do this. We would show up for church service, go through the motions, and then head home. I never heard anyone pray for increased clientele or income or guidance on a business decision. As I grow closer to God, I realize how much I need to include the Lord in my business. This has become a consistent habit I am doing, and I am finding that He is sending clients who are very strong in their faith. Some of my clients and I even pray together during appointments.

In addition, God guides me with every decision I need to make for my business. I share this with you because I want to encourage you to ask Him for guidance if you are not sure what to do in your business. Recently, I had lunch with a friend who has grown children, and she is trying to determine what she would like to do for a business. My friend shared that she had recently looked over a journal she did years ago, and the business idea she had was almost the same as the one she had had years ago. She was concerned that she was boxing herself into one type of person she would be helping and was not sure if her message should only be for those clients. We talked about how she has felt that God had placed it in her heart for some time now and was not sure how to proceed. Based on the demographics she wanted to serve and message she was going to offer, I suggested she volunteer at a local charity that worked with her ideal clientele. This would allow her to be sure that the message she had in her heart matched the need, and then she could offer it up to God for confirmation.

Looking back at when I started my business, I am glad that I chose something that I'm passionate about and that allows me to make an impact on my community. This brings me great joy because I am well known (sometimes too well) for my commitment to helping others in our program through scholarships.

When you start your business, you will find your mission and goals change and evolve. My goals over the last six years of being in business have changed from one year to the next. Originally, I started out with my first goal of being in the business of taking care of the clients using one product. The last four years have been a learning process of understanding that I have more to offer than just a product, that business is not always on the upswing, and that I need to always be reviewing my goals.

I have been blessed while being in business for myself to be able to help a charity that is dear to my heart called The Sylvia Thomas Center for Adoptive and Foster Families They help families that are adopting or are foster parents. So remember when you are looking at your business to ask yourself how you are paying it forward. You do not need to brag or advertise it. Just give, and the rewards you reap will be amazing.

Are you thinking of starting a business? Have you gotten to know the demographics of the area you will be working in? Are you familiar with the prices of your competitor's products and services? Keep in mind that being priced lower than your competition is not how you want to start your business. It is important to remember that you bring value to your service, and your time is money. Ensure that you can offer something more than or different from what your competition is offering and then price your product and services based on both product cost and the value of your time. You might find you will need to price yourself higher than your competition based on what you are providing your clients. Once your wrap your head around the value of your offering, you will see that your clients want, need, and love the options you give them. Consider incorporating packages and price them ending in the number seven ($197, $497 or $997), making sure they each offer something tangible. You will be surprised at your client retention. It is interesting how our mind wraps around the number seven and how often we go for the middle package.

Today I am in a place where I want to grow my business virtually and nationally. I want to hold on-site seminars for major corporations. I am currently thinking about what my next steps should be. Remember, we should always be looking for new ways to take our businesses to the next level. Recently, I have considered beginning to offer coaching via the internet or phone. I am looking at doing more with the guidance of my coach as I am setting up nationwide seminars, webinars, and virtual coaching. I know that there is a path set for me, and I will do my best to listen to what God places on my heart. As with all of us, our stories are always evolving, and my chapters are still being written.

The Painful Purpose

LYNN BROCKMAN

Life doesn't end just because you quit; so keep pushing.

"What would an abortion feel like?"

I sat silently in the dimly lit room just before dusk wondering if I should end this pregnancy before anyone would know. As I sat with my legs crossed on the floor of my bedroom, back against the wall, my head dropped into my hands in despair, abortion seemed like the easiest way to make this all go away, but it felt like the hardest obstacle to climb. Here I was, an 18-year-old high school student and pregnant. If I could have peeked into my future as a young girl, I would have never imagined this for my life. My thoughts were beginning to consume me as I kept vigil over this white stick with the two pink lines. Barely able to read the results because of the pending nightfall, I prayed that if I kept checking on it, one of the lines would magically disappear and my life could go back to "normal." Normal? What was normal anyway? I needed the kind of normal where the high school debutante was not an expectant mother. The kind of normal where the well-known cheerleader would not be sporting a baby bump in the coming months. I was praying for the kind of normal that would not disappoint my family because I had made a blind mistake that I would have to live with for the rest of my life. As I squinted my eyes in a last attempt to read the grade on the pregnancy test, it was official—I had failed.

The decision became crystal clear. I had to stop this pregnancy now so that I could have a chance at a better life later. There was a bright future ahead of me. I needed my education. My career goals included a six-figure salary. Neither of these came with a stroller and car seat attached to them. I had to devise a plan for today. I could see my future, and I already had a road map of how to accomplish my goals, but it didn't include my present situation. This gift that I was given came with many strings. Aside from my family woes, there was this guy whom I loved. Would he be upset if I told him that I was pregnant? How would he react if he found out that I had been pregnant but aborted his baby without his knowledge or consent? There were so many questions but very few answers. Even the more obvious outcomes appeared to be skewed at various moments throughout my thought process. I was confused. The one thing that was apparent was that I couldn't do this alone. No matter what decision I made, I would need help.

As early as I can remember, I would watch my mother in awe as she dressed for an event. I would watch her pace back and forth gathering garments from about the room to complete a look she had imagined in her head. She took special care in each part of her wardrobe to include the perfume choice. Her appearance was always intricately put together. She was very careful to pair her dress with what seemed to be the perfect high heels. On many occasions, she would allow me to add my input on accessories to adorn her well-thought-out outfit. I would open her jewelry box, which seemed to be more like a treasure chest, and sort through the metals and stones that adorned the dresser. It was more fascinating to be able to touch the jewels than to do the actual task at hand, but I performed them both with pride. It was a huge accomplishment for me to assist with completing my mother's look because I knew that she did not need my help, but it felt good to be able to give it. This was my first glimpse into my future. After graduating high school, I learned that I had a passion for fashion. With that, I decided to start my career in retail. It was wonderful! I was able to help others dress themselves properly. I monopolized on those intimate moments with my mom and used what she had taught me about style, material, and fashion to help others. It brought me joy to study my customer, identify their fashion needs, and add a smile to their wardrobe as they discovered clothing that fit and flattered their physique.

Most memorable were the ladies who were looking for an outfit for a special occasion. Many of them would have an idea of what they were looking for, and it began and ended with a little black dress. While every complete wardrobe should include several black pieces, I challenged myself to search beyond the obvious for clothing that appealed to a softer, gentler side of the customer. It was always exciting to experience that moment when the dressing room door would slowly open and a show of twirling began amongst a smile that only an oral surgeon could appreciate. It was undoubtedly apparent when the customer was impressed with their newly found treasure by the spins in the mirror to admire the panoramic view of themselves in their new outfit. To complete the look, I ripped a page from my mom's book and chose accessories that embellished and enhanced the final result. Although there were no bells and whistles that went off at the conclusion of this endeavor, I remember feeling that same sense of accomplishment when I was a child that made the difference for me. I was able to open a fashion door for women who lived inside of a very comfortable box. They rarely operated outside of those compounds because they did not know if it was safe to do so. My responsibility was to introduce their minds to a different way of life. It did not take long before I had mastered my craft and needed to move on. I knew that I had found my purpose, but it had to be cultivated and nurtured. I just had no idea on how to do that.

My fashion career began at some of the more moderately priced stores, but quickly progressed to the very high-end luxury clothing chains. I found myself in positions of management, overseeing as many as 150 employees at one time. At first, I was disappointed that I would not be able to engage in my one-on-one customer exchanges that I had grown fond of. Leadership carried a different responsibility. In order to fulfill my need to assist the customers, I began to teach the employees how to help them. I poured years of experience that I had gathered along my journey into those associates who were open to learning. There were some bumps and bruises that I had received during my ride that I adjusted and warned of so that they would not make the same mistakes. Before long, my employees were able to discover a customer's clothing size before it was given, determine which parts of a body to accentuate and which to cover up, and how to approach patrons with caution. Their education sessions equated to more money for the company. More money for the company meant recognition on a job well done. I took those accolades and hit the road running. I was asked to oversee several stores in different states. My title grew from General Manager to District Manager and later, Regional Manager. This new opportunity was very challenging in the beginning, but I knew that perseverance would prove to be a powerful tool if I just remained focused and determined.

Growing up in a small town did not afford me the luxury of traveling much. All that I knew of life happened close to home. It was extremely rare that my family and I would travel to other states because most of the family lived in the same area in which we were raised. Now, here I was, near the top of the food chain and flying several times a week. I traveled to different target areas to provide suggestions on how to increase profits. It was my responsibility to ensure that each store was working to its full potential. I researched the financial output of the stores, gathered pertinent data on employees and the surrounding companies, and compiled an analysis on how to gain financial success in that region. My hard work and dedication paid off. I was promoted to overseeing the majority of accounts for a very high-end retail chain within the US. It became exciting to assist in setting the fashion trends that influenced the nation. I was making a difference.

Additionally, I sat in on board meetings among the stakeholders to advise on how stores in varying markets could improve their productivity. Here I was, little ole me, making millions of dollars for this company. It baffled me at times when I felt unfulfilled in my career. I knew that I was giving my job all of my energy because the numbers said so. My purpose was being met because I was helping people on a different level. The scared little girl sitting in a room all alone contemplating big girl decisions was now traveling the country and was viewed as an expert in the fashion industry. How could I be lacking anything at this point? Wasn't helping others what I desired to do? Why was I feeling lost when I was dominating the field of retail?

On those days of mental emptiness, I often think back to that day when fear gripped my world and propelled me into my destiny. The low point in my life was that very day in my bedroom. In the pit of my stomach, I can still feel the desperation and depression I felt on that day as my mind swayed back and forth, up and down, like a seesaw. That very moment of immobilization usually helps me to appreciate the upward climb that I've had to endure. Fear has a way of paralyzing us and keeping us stagnant, but we have to take every ounce of strength and tenacity that we own to thrust ourselves forward into our calling. These feelings of inadequacy can cause us to lose track of our goals or refocus them unnecessarily. On the other hand, we can take that discomfort and use it as an asset. It can push us closer to obtaining our goals. As I sat in the dark on that gloomy evening contemplating life or death, I realized that I had the power to change my situation into a positive one. I chose life. Surprisingly, my family embraced and supported my pregnancy. Instead of ending the life of my unborn child, I became the proud mother (and now a grandmother) of a baby girl. I wish I could say that life was happily ever after, but it wasn't. There were some growing pains along my journey that I was able to conquer. It took strong prayers to get through some of the issues that I faced, but I made it. It was both difficult and rewarding, but I am very happy with the decisions that I made.

Although I had a strong interest in fashion, I felt like I needed something else. There was a longing to help more and to do more. I had sold clothes, shoes, and accessories, but there was a gaping hole within me that was yearning to be filled. As I started to reevaluate my career goals, I knew that I had not even scratched the surface of how to make the people around me feel beautiful. Dressing them was the easy part, but helping them to learn true beauty from the inside was lacking. I began to put together a plan on how to reach customers and fulfill them from the inside out. Convincing upper-level management to lend retail hours to counsel the patrons fell in the pile of "parked ideas" to be addressed at a later date. The retail industry had policies and procedures to adhere to, and it prevented me from diving under the layers of low self-esteem. I needed to have an in-depth conversation with the customers, but I was told on several occasions that time would not permit such an interaction. However, it was important for me to dress up the inside as well as the outside. I needed to transform the customers. The biggest issue was how to accomplish this with consent from upper-level management. It was a huge challenge to get them to even listen to the idea. I urged that our focus should have been on shaping the inner person, but it wasn't. Clothes were being sold to cover up the real issues. After several doors were shut on the notion, I created a platform for men and women to begin to search within for beauty. The birth of UGLYDollFace, Entertainment was phenomenal.

U Gotta Love Yourself, Entertainment runs the gamut in the fashion world. We have mastered the art of beauty. Of course, we focus on clothing as one aspect of the organization. However, we do not stop there. UGLYDollFace is excited to offer every realm of beauty and entertainment, from counseling to performing arts to unique office space and decor. We offer services that meet the needs of our clients on many levels. We believe that if you can dream it, then we will devise a plan to achieve it.

I know what you're asking. It's the million-dollar question. Why is a company that encourages fashion and beauty called ugly? I have had countless debates on changing the name, but I have held firm. The name has meaning. It tells the story of how someone with so much potential can view themselves in a very negative light. Fortunately, the story doesn't end with the sun going down. There is always a tomorrow and a brighter day ahead. As we know, dolls are usually very attractive. Therefore, you can be nice, shiny, and new on the outside, but you don't know what a person is suffering through on the inside. While there may be challenges on one day, if you keep at it, things will turn around. In essence, the things that are viewed as negative can be your positive outlook tomorrow. It is important that we appreciate all aspects of ourselves. Long legs, thick hips, and large torsos do not have to be negative aspects. Don't view things that don't look like the norm as undesirable. It may actually be a prize, so appreciate what was given to you. Enjoy your today, but consider your tomorrow. Rejoice in knowing that you are a doll.

I took some very basic concepts and developed it into a company. We are making dreams come true. We are the frontrunners in rejuvenating your wardrobe. Our goal is to set the stage and foundation in customer service without covering up the truth. Once the internal and external transformation is complete, we offer an array of other services. UGLYDollFace has managed to merge retail and entertainment under one umbrella. Therefore, we are able to assist with projects that require studio time. We are excited to work with musicians, poets, and the like in accomplishing their professional and personal goals. We have staff members who are able to provide clear and concise directions on obtaining your musical goals. Our only options for results are success.

Now the questions become what was all of this for? What is the purpose of the struggle? Was it worth it?

I feel that life is made up of several tests. Those are the hiccups along your journey. You may have a plan and direction for your life, but things don't always go as planned. You have to be prepared for those moments when a speed bump is placed in your way. I had a plan on how my life would go. My speed bump was my unplanned pregnancy. I didn't know it then, but there was still a life worth living after having a baby. It may not have been the ideal situation, but I survived. Trust me, there were many days where I not only contemplated taking the life of my unborn child but also my own life. I felt like life was not going well and not worth continuing. That hiccup is my strength. I know that feeling of loneliness and desperation too well, and I never want another human being to experience it. There are truly bells, whistles, and sirens on the other side of pain. We just have to get to it.

After the test is the testimony. We get the chance to tell our story. My chapter could have ended at 18. The only thing that my friends and family would have been able to say about me is that I appeared to be a normal teenager. Normal? There was absolutely nothing normal about me. However, I used all of my pain, all of my heartache, and all of my grief to push me to be better. Deep inside, I knew that I was born with a purpose. I knew that I was here to make a difference. Had I possessed enough courage to attempt the suicide that plagued my thoughts, I may have taken many people with me. I have met people who are encouraged and inspired when they get a beauty transformation or a talk that empowers them. Without that stimulated whisper to my customers, some of them may not have made it through their own test. I know that I was an integral part of their success.

Yes, it was difficult. Yes, I felt unworthy. Yes, I put on a façade. But it was worth it. I am a much better person because of it. I can speak to my customers from experience and not a from textbook. Transforming lives comes easier because I have a proven method that works.

UGLYDollFace is helping others go to the next level. They are able to hold their heads up a little higher and tread lighter. I feel overwhelming success when I leave a customer with a winning smile on their face. It brings me joy to imagine how they will take the information that they obtained and transform the next person to be who they were born to be. We can be a nation helping each other get out of the dark and gloomy rooms called depression. We can progress and push forward to what we know is the best. Together, we can stand strong and encourage each other through our storms. We can't do it alone, and now we don't have to. UGLYDollFace will get you great results when you allow us to lead the way.

God's Vision, My Decision, and His Provision

CHERYL POLOTE-WILLIAMSON

*"For I know the thoughts that I think toward you,
says the LORD, thoughts of peace and not of evil, to
give you a future and a hope."*
—Jeremiah 29:11 NKJV

success
noun | suc·cess | sǝk-'ses

1) outcome, result
2 a) degree or measure of succeeding
   b) favorable or desired outcome; also, the attainment of wealth, favor, or eminence
3) one that succeeds

As you can see from looking at the definition of the word *success*, there is more than one way to describe exactly what it is. To some people, it means reaching a certain position in their career at a company. To others, it may mean being an entrepreneur. For someone else, it may mean owning a certain type of car or living in a certain neighborhood. Some may feel that success is determined by reaching a certain level of education. For others, it may mean having a family. These interpretations represent varied aspects of success.

Thus, no one's definition or idea of success is wrong. *What does success mean to you?* I encourage you to take a few moments to think carefully about this and write your answer(s) on a piece of paper. You and *only* you have the power to define what success looks like in *your* life. After all, how can you truly succeed if you don't even know what *you* deem successful?

Regardless of your background, upbringing, socioeconomic status, race, color, or creed—you can be successful! Know that if you are diligent and determined to be successful, you *will* be! There is no limited edition or scarce quantity of success reserved only for an elite, selected few. It is my personal belief that success is leaving an indelible mark on the world. I believe impact is made by serving, giving, and helping those who are unable or perhaps unwilling to help themselves. As a second-generation entrepreneur, my definition of success also includes operating a successful business, and I am so grateful that I have had the opportunity to do so. I'll share more about some of my experiences as a serial entrepreneur later in this chapter.

I am passionate about entrepreneurship because I watched my father build his construction company from the ground up. Entrepreneurship also provides me with the resources and flexibility to help people. Being that I am in business for myself, I am in control of my time, and therefore I can do more, serve more, and impact more. My desire is to serve and impact others by showing them that success is for everyone. Regardless of *how* you define success, it is important to know that there are many factors that play a part in how you attain it. It is also crucial that anyone with entrepreneurial aspirations understands that being a business owner is not always as glamorous as it seems. Please do not be fooled into thinking that entrepreneurship is about ten-hour work weeks and two-week-long vacations. If this is your expectation of business ownership, do yourself a favor and stop now, because you are in for a rude awakening! I'm not saying this to frighten you. I just want to paint a realistic picture so that you know firsthand what is in store when you decide that you want to be in business for yourself. Below, I have outlined five success factors that have proven to be game changers in my serial entrepreneurial efforts. When I started making each of these things part of my daily life, my business grew exponentially, and my brand became solidified. Most importantly, my mindset began to transform. I encourage you to read each factor carefully and take notes.

Success Factor #1: Research, Research, Research

Being knowledgeable about the ins and outs of your business is absolutely the most important piece of advice that I give my coaching clients. If you aren't knowledgeable about your business, how can you conduct business? Also, if you are not a bona fide expert on your business, how can clients trust you enough to support you? Become well acquainted with the Small Business Administration (SBA). The SBA is a government agency that offers numerous avenues of support to entrepreneurs and small businesses. Take advantage of the resources available to you. Go to the library and check out books about your business interest. Be obsessive about learning all that you can. Do you know someone who is currently involved in the type of business that you are interested in? Take them to lunch or ask them if you can shadow them for a day. Google is your friend. These days, you can find information on just about any and everything. There is nothing holding you back from becoming an expert in your field.

Think outside of the box as far as how you can gain information. For example, maybe it means taking a part-time job at a company that is already in the business that you are hoping to build. This will provide you with direct access to valuable and pertinent information. Don't make the mistake of thinking that you should always pay for knowledge. Of course, there are situations in which you will have to. For example, if your goal requires you to earn a degree or certification, it will be necessary for you to pay for the knowledge that you need. However, there are plenty of free resources available. It's up to you to take advantage of them. Always exhaust *all* free options before paying for knowledge. Plan and budget accordingly if you know that you will need to pay for certifications or licensing.

You also need know how to do every job in your company. In my days as a franchise owner of five Title Boxing clubs, one of the first things I remember was having to know how to do every job from being a cashier to selling memberships to teaching classes when necessary. For example, I had to step in for an instructor for a 5:00am class at one point. As the business owner, I had a difficult choice to make. I had to decide whether I would allow a poor customer service experience for those members who were expecting to have a class that morning or to step up and make sure that I was there to cover. I chose the latter. It was not easy nor was it convenient for me, but I did it because that's what entrepreneurship is about; it's about sacrifice and making the tough decisions.

Success Factor #2: Make a Vision Board

I am a firm believer in the power of vision boards because I am a living example of what they can do. A couple of years ago, I created a vision board, and one of the things on my board was that I wanted to be an international speaker and a bestselling author. At the time, I had no clue how that idea would come to fruition. Believe it or not, I was terrified at the very thought of speaking in front of people. I didn't know the first thing about writing a book or having it published; I can't even type! How was I going to write a book if I could not even type?! Seeing my goals posted on my vision board every day caused me to be laser focused on finding a way to make things happen. Before I knew it, God got behind my efforts and provided all the people and the resources that I needed to publish my book. He also gave me the courage that I needed to find my voice and conquer my fear of public speaking. I am now proud to say that I can easily speak to a room full of thousands of people. This is an example of the awesome power of God *and* the power of a vision board.

If you are skeptical about whether vision boards really work, I challenge you to give it a try. I only speak on things that have worked for me, and I know that since my vision board has helped me bring things to pass, creating a vision board can do the same for you. So, how do you create a vision board? It starts with having a vision. You must know where you want to go and what you want to accomplish. Take some time to write three of your main goals and think about the necessary steps that you will need to take to make them a reality. Once you've done that, you have a good starting point for your vision. From there, you can create your vision board. All you need to create your vision board is scissors, tape or glue, poster board, and some magazines. Cut out pictures, words, and articles that align with your vision. Once you have created your vision board, hang it somewhere you will see it every single day.

Success Factor #3: Persevere and Be Willing to Sacrifice

It may sound cliché, but success is not for the faint of heart. Specifically, if your idea of success includes being in business for yourself, you must learn how to persevere. Your faith and your patience will be tried and tested along your journey to success, but you must remember that you are not alone. Staying focused and seeing your vision board daily can help with this when the going gets tough. At Title, there were times when I had no money left after paying my employees, which meant that there was no money to give myself a salary. Most business owners do not make a salary in their first year of operation. *Is this something that you are willing to accept?* If I had quit because I was not able to pay myself, this book would not have been published. If I had quit then, there would be no multiple bestselling author status. My point is that you can't quit just because things are not easy.

I had to make numerous sacrifices as a business owner. I remember receiving holiday photos from my family back home in Savannah, GA and feeling overwhelmed with emotions because I wasn't there. I couldn't spend the holidays with my family because I had a business to run. I was focused and determined to make my business a success, and that came with heavy costs. Sometimes that cost was not going home to see my family for the holidays. Sometimes that cost was missing my kids' soccer games and track meets. Sometimes that cost was not being able to have lunch with friends. Sometimes that cost was losing friends because of multiple missed dates and events. Sometimes that cost was having to cancel a vacation at the last minute because the staff members who were supposed to cover me were no longer available. Sometimes that cost was self-doubt and constantly wondering if I made the wrong decision by choosing to own my business. This self-doubt would lead to feelings of loneliness and depression. Sometimes the cost was working when I was sick or putting in fourteen-hour days for weeks at a time.

I experienced a myriad of emotions during my time as fitness club owner, but I learned many valuable lessons about entrepreneurship and about myself. I learned how to persevere and how to work tirelessly toward accomplishing my goals. After three years of owning the boxing clubs, I felt led to move in another direction—being an author and inspirational speaker. When I saw how my first book touched people, I knew that I was onto something, and I knew that I wanted to do more. From there, Cheryl Polote-Williamson, LLC was born. Building my brand and turning my personal pain into profit has proven to be challenging at times, too. I've wondered if I've shared too much personal information in my books. I've wondered if people would be able to relate to and connect with my story. My journey has certainly not been an easy one, but I wouldn't change a thing.

According to serial entrepreneur and *New York Times* bestselling author, Gary Vaynerchuk, perseverance is a major part of his equation for success in his business. In a recent article in *Entrepreneur* magazine, Vaynerchuk said "A 'wannapreneur' quits and gets a job after the first punch in the face. An entrepreneur can take unlimited punches and build a business that lasts." Ask yourself, "Am I in this for the long haul, or am I simply pursuing a fleeting idea?" If you are in it for the long haul, know that you are going to take some punches and you are going to fail at some things. Don't let this shake your confidence. Pick yourself up, dust yourself off, and try again. Need more convincing that you should roll with the punches when it comes to entrepreneurship? Walt Disney was fired from his job at a newspaper before he created Disney World, which is now worth $35 billion. Steve Jobs was fired from Apple Computers before leading the company to be one of the most successful and most recognizable brands in our nation's history; Apple is now worth $750 billion. Thomas Edison tried over 10,000 times before finally inventing the light bulb. Fred Smith, the founder of Fed Ex, wrote about his idea for the delivery company in a college essay. His professor at the time said that his idea was "interesting but not feasible." Fed Ex is now worth

$52.3 billion. Lastly and certainly not least, as she is one of my role models, Oprah Winfrey was fired from her job at a Baltimore news station before starting her career as one of the most notable media figures of our time. Her net worth is currently $2.7 billion.

Success Factor #4: Set Up Your Business Properly

This is another thing that I tell clients often; if you are going to be in business, be in business! Ensure that you have the proper business systems in place. For example, you should have a business bank account that is separate from your personal account. You should also have a business email address that is not connected to your personal email. Be sure that you have a tax identification number and that your business is registered with the state. If you have employees, use an actual payroll service to pay them. These may seem like trivial things, but they can become significant issues if your business is ever audited or when it is time for you to seek investors.

When I first got started as business owner, I realized that I didn't have my business set up properly. I learned that not doing so could potentially put my household in jeopardy. Thankfully, I learned what needed to be done early on and was able to set up the systems that I needed to. Don't make small mistakes that could have major repercussions down the line. Check with your state about licensing, insurance, and liabilities for business owners.

Success Factor #5: Know the Importance of Relational Currency

I saved this success factor for last because it is perhaps the most important of them all. When I discovered how crucial relational currency was and began practicing it regularly, my business changed for the better. Relational or relationship currency is establishing a personal connection that goes beyond a simple business transaction. For example, if I want to do business with someone, I look at them as more than just a potential business partner. When I started putting forth the time and effort to develop relationships with the people I work with, I noticed a positive change in my business dealings with them.

A major part of relational currency is serving. You should never ask for something from someone before you have served them. For example, I found a way to begin serving someone whom I looked up to. I wanted her to be my mentor. I served her for two years before asking anything of her. Eventually, she asked me what she could do for me. By giving generously of my time and resources, I established strong relational currency with her, and she and I both reaped the benefits. Focus on building relationships with people with whom you work or want to work. Most importantly, never be too busy to serve others.

Cheryl Polote-Williamson, LLC was not created overnight or by osmosis. My business and my brand are direct results of God's vision, my decision to go after my dreams, and God's provision. Your journey to success will not be an easy one, and I'm not here to convince you that everything is going to be perfect. I am here to convince you that the journey will be full of uncertainties and unpleasantries, but the destination will be so worth it. Stay encouraged and eradicate your life and business of all negative energies. Protect your vision and keep your goals at the forefront of your mind at all times. Stay focused and surround yourself with people who are walking out their definitions of success. You can do it because God gave you the necessary tools when He created you. He equipped you with the capacity to handle everything that will come your way. I am happy that you have chosen to take the road less traveled and strive for excellence in your pursuit of success.

My Gems of Success

NANCY FULLER GARLAND

I was born Nancy Denise Fuller on December 3 (you don't need to know the year) to Herman and Maggie Lene Stepp Fuller (maiden name Stepp has a story behind it). I was born in Pittsburgh, Pennsylvania. We lived there until I was six years old and then moved to Hopkinsville, Kentucky. I was placed in the second grade at an all-black school. The school I attended up to the eighth grade was called Durrett Avenue. From that school, I was slated to attend Attucks High School (another all-black school) beginning in the ninth grade. The year was 1968, and low and behold, the schools were integrated in the small town of Hopkinsville. My parents divorced when I was twelve years old. I remember talking to my father around that age. He was rarely around. He was in the military, and I did not travel with him. Yet, I adored him. I loved and respected my mother, but to a daughter, a father is special, and he was in my eyes. He was so well groomed, and one of the things I remember most is his clean finger nails. I guess it seemed to me that the men I was aware of, while hard working, were often dirty from their jobs, many of which were in construction. I can remember also as a young girl my father playing the flute to Johnny Mathis. My father also painted oil paintings of my mother.

All of that was lost when I was very young. I was still in grade school, and I don't remember the exact age, but our home caught on fire, and all of our family pictures of him and our baby pictures were gone. My father was in Germany at the time and sent us an album of pictures of him and our baby pictures. For years, I could not stand to hear the sound of a fire truck without feeling anxiety. We went to reside with my grandmother, who was really my mother's paternal grandmother. Both my mother's parents were deceased by the time she was three. She was reared by her father's mother. Everything was lost in that fire. I remember that Christmas, my sister Darlene and I received Raggedy Ann dolls. We always had food and clothing, but by the standards of that time, we were living in poverty.

I did experience some bullying in high school, which I remember to this day. I had the normal challenges in life that most people have. I graduated high school in 1971 and college in 1978, mostly because while my father was not around most of the time, my mother certainly was. If there was anyone on God's green earth I feared, it was my mother. She was very strict, so once I had some freedom, I was a party animal, but I was so young. I was a senior in high school at sixteen and turned seventeen in December. In college, I pledged Delta Sigma Theta Sorority Inc. I met my first husband in college. We dated for three years and were married for fifteen. The marriage failed for a number of reasons. Each of us was to blame for the demise of our marriage, but we have a beautiful daughter who is a God-fearing human being whom we both cherish. I wish I could talk about my great work in the church, but I cannot.

I have always believed in God. After all, my mother and her grandmother are buried on church grounds of

West Union Baptist Church. I sat on what was called the mourning bench in that church while the preacher preached. The deacons prayed and would sing hymns. For the life of me, I couldn't understand why it would take thirty minutes to sing one line. I was baptized, and it was truly like the painting "The Baptism." We marched to the river with church members on the bank in our gowns. Swimming caps led down to the bank where the ministers and the deacons were waiting, praying over and truly baptizing in the river. I have always been spiritual and have always understood the presence of the spirit of our savior. Even as a youngster, I understood that I could not and still cannot quote Bible verses. I truly believe that is a gift, one that I don't have. My grandmother gave us children's Bible stories book as soon as I was able to read. I had a praying grandmother and mother. I have pictures of both of my mother and grandmother at about the age of fourteen. What a wonderful blessing to have two generations belong to the same church.

One thing I found out is that how you are reared affects who you are and how you are. Poverty has its own effects. Lack of parents, parents who are awful, lack of self-esteem and self-confidence. Also, abuse, sexual, mental and emotional or all of the above. For me, I had daddy issues for years. I questioned, wondered, and speculated as to how a father could abandon four children and take my mother's maiden name just to get back into the military. He married another woman while still married to my mother. He gave his new wife and the daughter they had together my mother's name. They traveled between Germany and Pittsburgh, and she had no idea what his birth name was. Imagine that. He was something else. I did see my father on occasions, and although I was not there, I'm told he cheated on her frequently. I sure hope this apple fell far from the tree.

When I became an adult, I understood that his lack of love or responsibility had nothing to do with me. I now understand there was a large void within him that he continued to fill with all the wrong things. These kind of deficits can be filled by one thing and one thing only, and this is the Holy Spirit. I never truly had a father, but I always wanted one.

I want to talk about my mother, who was one of the most intelligent and wisest people I have ever known. While the artistry may have come from my father, the strength, desire to succeed, character, and whatever wisdom I may possess came from her. She married at sixteen, and nine months and three days later, she gave birth to me. (I know, I checked.) She was seventeen years old. She told me a funny story about how when I was being potty-trained, her cabinet with her pots and pans were ground level, and I would urinate in anything that looked like a pot to me. Needless to say, she would check them. But I digress. Although she was young, the role of mother and child were always clear and distinct. She reared four children mostly on her own and ruled us not with corporal punishment (although there was some of that) but with the sheer will of her personality. I saw a documentary once on television regarding kids who did not use drugs, and all of them stated that their parents would kill them. I remember laughing and thinking that I knew how they felt. As I look back on it, I know she would not have killed us, but we needed to believe she would, and we did. Thanks, mama.

I wondered what inspires one to begin a business. Is it the opportunity to make a lot of money? The desire to share a talent? A push from the Holy Spirit? A powerful love from someone? A calling? An accident? I didn't begin to write this until I was on a cruise ship. There are a couple of reasons I procrastinated. The first one was I wasn't sure what direction I wanted to go. The second and the most important was I was waiting on the Holy Spirit to move me. Like most human beings, I have faced some adversities. Luckily, I have not had to endure any sexual abuse or domestic violence. Now emotional abuse or mental abuse is a different matter. Those types of things often make us mean spirited. The main things I have learned is there is true power in positive thinking. I never really believed it until I began to notice that if I put positive thoughts and images in my mind, they were just as likely to come to fruition as the negative ones.

Why am I in business? It was never my intent to be in business. I would save my money in anticipation of buying some precious necklaces from Neiman Marcus. One day, a very dear friend of mine by the name of Constance Barron Wilson invited me to an international gem and jewelry show. The show comes twice a year to Dallas, TX and is usually held at the Market Hall. From the moment I entered through those glass doors, I was totally enthralled. Oh my! The jewels and the beads! So much to choose from. So much diversity in quality and price. As I was walking down the aisle, I happened to notice some of the same beads in a necklace I purchased. At that moment, and only God knows why, I decide to purchase that strand of beads to make my very own necklace. That day, I purchased several strands of beads. I remember it like it was yesterday, and this was over ten years ago. I bought jade, garnet, crystal, mother of pearl, and amethyst. I also purchased all types of citrine, turquoise, amber, emeralds, ruby, chalcedony, opal, agate, aquamarine, coral, carnelian, druzy, hematite, and howlite, just to name a few. What a day and what a memory that was. I was home in my heart and in my mind. Now having said all that, I had no idea what I was doing. I purchased some fishing wire, beads, and crimps and figured it out. At first, I would sit up all night in bed creating.

I was so happy and excited. I had an acquaintance who worked at the flea market, and I showed her some of my work. I was just sharing my work with her, and she stated that she knew the owners of an art gallery called Heliotrope. The night of the gallery show, two of my pieces sold. I was an unknown artist who sold three strand necklaces for well over two hundred dollars. I could not believe that I sold pieces without having met the owners. Both owners turned out to be wonderful people. Heliotrope has since closed.

The other person who believed in me from the very beginning owns Adair Optical. These are events that I never actually sought out. God directed them. I have been in magazines like *360 West* and *Indulge* more than once. Once, *Indulge* asked to use a necklace in their magazine shoot. Little did I know, it would be on a Ford model on the cover of the magazine. That necklace sold the next day for six hundred and five dollars. Every time I would become discouraged, God would send me a sign. He would constantly reaffirm my calling, path, direction—whatever you would like to call it. I began to do shows at private residences, but also at the Fort Worth Club, Colleyville Women's Club, The Winery, The Link's Organization, Maverick Fine Western Wear, and Leddy's, to name a few. I have had two great marketing teams: LGR Group and Anchor Marketing. I have a great website and logo. I have a wonderful YouTube video created by Anchor Marketing and have appeared on several radio shows. I also had the pleasure of showing pieces at the Annual Mary Kay Convention at the Kate Baily Hutchinson Convention Center.

My family has been extremely supportive by purchasing pieces from me and coming to my shows and events. When I received the award for one the top 25 women of Dallas given by the Steed Society, I could not believe it. Again, God was sending me encouragement and telling me not to despair. When I first began my business, some friends laughed at my idea of starting a jewelry line. Others complained about the size of some of my pieces. I finally had to stop trying to please those critics and instead design what I was meant to. I focus on what inspires me, and I knew those who under-stood my artistry would appreciate and purchase it. I also learned that those who love you support you but also tell you the truth. I have had many people help me.

I remember one time I was in church, and my pastor announced that he was giving five hundred dollars to assist some of his church members who had small businesses. What a blessing that turned out to be for me. It enabled me to buy products that I needed. Sometimes my heart would be so heavy, not just about business, but other issues in this journey called life. I would go to my studio and create all day, and sometimes all night. It calmed me. I experienced creative focus. In the midst of all this, God sent me a business partner whom I will always hold in my heart as my own personal angel. When someone believes in you and puts their money where their mouth is, it gives affirmation more than encouragement. It gives you strength and purpose, which I certainly needed. Several occurrences happened after the partnerships, including awards, features in magazines, and a Fox 4 News segment about me and my business.

As I continue to design and make one-of-a-kind artistic pieces (mostly necklaces), I pray for success. I truly dream of being in a position to help others. I am a big advocate of education and for domestic violence victims.

"Therefore I tell you, whatever you ask for in prayer, believe that you have received it, and it will be yours."

— Mark 11:24, NIV

I know this will happen because I have faith. I pray daily for things seen and unseen, known and unknown, possible and impossible, because it all centers on one thing and one thing only, and that is God.

Like all artists I have ever known, I just want to do the art. I used to wonder how singers and other artists go bankrupt. They are the talent. Let me tell you, the talent makes the least amount of money. Everyone else gets paid first. You have to pay the vendors, the marketing teams, the website designers, and your employees. You have to pay for travel, hotels, rent, food, and a thousand other expenses you don't even think about. I have come to the conclusion that God gives an artist love for the art and not the money. Otherwise I am sure we would have a lot less of it. Again, there is the need for validation. To know and really believe what you do is relevant and good. God always sent someone or a sign to remind me I was on the path on which I am meant to be.

Most of my jewelry is named after people who have supported and inspired me. This allows me to show my customers appreciation. I have met many wonderful people from all over the world and made great business relationships and friendships. Often people ask what inspires me. It's often just a feeling. It could be from seeing a certain color, designing in my mind, or discussing an idea with a friend. There is no set guide to inspiration. Just being alive and a child of God is inspiration enough. Poverty inspired me to buy shoes. As a child, my dress shoes always had to be black, and I promised myself that when I grew up, I would have many pairs of shoes of all colors. Of course, I was inspired to make necklaces to complement my shoes that are in my private collection.

Now, to who am I and who I want to be. They are not always the same thing, but in this instance, they are. I believe myself to be a flawed human being, and I have all the negative baggage that comes with that. I have a deep sense of friendship and loyalty and take both seriously. I try to live a decent life and believe it's my duty to set an example for younger women. I am a wife and mother, and I believe I do the best I can. Am I always successful? Probably not. But I persevere. I have learned to love myself first and foremost. I believe the only true value of money is for what it can buy.

I believe in living and not just existing. I also want everyone around me to be happy, and if not, at least be in the pursuit of it. Know this—fear is the true enemy. It has taken me a long time to understand that it's okay for me to be happy, to have success, and to receive help. On occasions when I feel fear, I tell Satan to get behind me. The God I serve is mighty and will never forsake me. As I write this, I claim all that is meant to be for me and for you.

My last suggestions:

1. Do as the spirit guides you.
2. Be kind to others.
3. Lie to others if you must but never lie to yourself.
4. Know yourself.
5. Know the only person you can control is yourself.
6. Never forget who is truly in charge. It is not you. It is God.
7. Last but not least, HOLD ON TO YOUR DREAMS!

Success Is Happiness

KAMERON JONES-MARZETTE

"Success isn't always about greatness. It's about consistency. Consistent hard work leads to success. Greatness will come."
–Dwayne Johnson

"If we risk nothing, we risk everything."
—Geena Davis

"Mom, you are my inspiration." Those were the words that my daughter said to me during one of our random conversations, which now is a faint memory to me. I only recall those five little words that she said. Hearing them come from her mouth made my heart sing with delight because I immediately thought, "Well, I must be doing something right!" The fact of the matter is I've always been my own worst critic. While that wasn't the first time I'd heard someone express that form of endearment to me, on that day when my child said it, it meant something more. My daughter meant those words because she had been with me through all of my struggles and sacrifice. Despite it all and because of it all, she believed in me.

I often think back to some dark periods in my life when those words would have helped me to feel like less of a failure. The crisp persona that I was known for was really a person struggling with a great deal of self-doubt and worry on the inside. My success path was often clouded by this muddled view. When I was alone in my thoughts, I measured myself against what other women possessed or what they had going on in their lives. For some reason in my mind, I felt like I always came up short. Failure can be good preparation for success, but that's only a fraction of my story. I've actually experienced success in several areas of my life. I have had strong relationships, educational achievements, and a solid career. The problem was that I never viewed those things as successes. I viewed them more as the results of what I had spent my life working hard for. I secretly wanted more, and I just didn't know that greatness was in my path.

I started thinking about success when a dear friend of mine contacted me on the phone. She had co-authored a book and she wanted to share the exciting news. I was blown away to hear of her accomplishment. After a few months passed, my friend's co-author experience was a huge success. I was so thrilled for her, and her success didn't surprise me. My friend is smart, talented, and driven. I could recognize those qualities in her, but I often overlooked them in myself. As I celebrated with her over the phone, I could only think of how proud I was of her. I had no idea that a few months later, this same friend would approach me about a being a co-author in a book as well. I felt honored to even be considered, yet I was eerily hesitant. Feelings of self-doubt filled my thoughts, and immediately, I started to wonder what I could bring to the project. I decided that before I could commit to it, I had to do some soul searching to re-define what success meant to me. I must admit, I had associated success with material things related to wealth and power. Wealthy and successful people typically have expensive things. While there is some truth to this thinking, deep down inside, I knew that success meant so much more. Success is a mindset, and personal success is individualized. It can't be measured or defined by what others have or what they are doing. Success comes from within, and it can present itself in various aspects of your life. I had to acknowledge that the areas of my life in which I felt most successful were also the parts of my life in which I felt the happiest. I agreed to share my story because I know the benefits of self-worth, consistency, and happiness. These elements lead to success and ultimately to a more fulfilled life.

My childhood prepared me to be a success. Growing up, I saw that hard work pays off, and I believed that being hardworking was an important quality to have. I watched my parents willingly go to work every day. My dad owned a successful business, and my mom was a highly respected nurse in her field. Hard work and consistency are what I learned because I saw them model these attributes every day. Being an only child, I was close to my parents. Daily conversations with my mom were very instrumental in helping me understand the importance of education. We would often talk about my day, and she would share hers with me. Her job sounded so interesting. As a child, I witnessed my parents going to jobs that they loved and that they were passionate about. This made me want to have a job that I loved, too. I would pretend that I had a job when I played with my Barbie dolls. My doll conversations sounded similar to the ones that I would have with my mom after school and work. My parents were consistent. I knew I could count on them. They were my role models growing up. To this day, even though my dad is in his 70s, he still works. He works because he loves what he does and it fulfills him. These early experiences helped me to understand the correlation between hard work and success. My parents were successful, and that helped me know that I would be successful too.

Achieving my educational goals is one area in which I have felt great success. I knew that education would help propel me toward my goals, but school wasn't always super easy for me. Math was a persistent problem area for me. I can remember getting nervous during many of my math classes as a young student because it wasn't a strength of mine. While I recognized this in elementary school, I still wanted to overcome my fear of math. These insecurities didn't change much when I entered high school. Geometry was one of the hardest subjects for me. Failing test score after failing score, I often felt disappointed in myself. It seemed like I was the only one struggling in the class. Despite having an unapproachable teacher who taught mainly to the students who got it, I didn't allow these setbacks discourage me. I worked with other students, obtained additional resources on the lessons, and mustered up the nerve to get help from my teacher. Before the convenience of the Internet, I was networking and utilizing my resources to help me succeed. I've always had a knack for problem solving because failure has never been an option in my mind.

My senior year was spent getting myself prepared to graduate and enter college. My grades were solid, so I wasn't too concerned that I might not be accepted into my school of choice. Disappointment loomed around the corner, though.

My college entrance exam scores turned out to be a little less than stellar. As the other students started buzzing about their scores, I secretly felt like a failure. I knew my scores weren't as good as I wanted them to be, and my anxiety about it was escalating. I hated that my fate for college might be solely dependent on a test score because I *knew* that I could excel at any school that I attended. The bad news showed up in the mail one day. I was not accepted into my college of choice. At the time, it seemed so unfair! I was so embarrassed and disappointed in myself that I tore the letter up. I didn't tell my parents or any of my friends that I hadn't been accepted. Instead, I immediately began applying to other colleges that I previously had no interest in. I was accepted into several, but I chose one that was close to home. Once I got that official letter of acceptance, I felt confident enough to share the good news with my parents. I was able to solve that problem completely on my own, and I never doubted that I would turn that setback into a success. I chose a new route, and I never once looked back. Three graduate degrees later, I would say that I am educationally fulfilled.

Another area where I feel immense success is in my personal relationships with others. I am especially proud of my job as a mother. I must say that this brings me the greatest sense of reward. My journey to motherhood got off to a rocky start. First, my pregnancy was unexpected. I got married shortly after college, and I immediately became pregnant. It all happened in the same year, so I had very little time to prepare for my role as a mother. I was still learning how to be a wife when I had to figure out how to be a mother as well. Selfish thoughts consumed me, but I gradually became more excited about the growing life inside of me. My difficult pregnancy left me on bedrest for weeks at a time. I often feared that I might lose my baby. Prayer and my faith in God got me through this challenging period. God answered my prayers. My daughter was born, and she was exactly what I had prayed for. What a feeling of joy that I had this precious little girl. She was born early in my new career. I was a new wife, and I was just beginning to further my graduate education. All of these things added great value to my life, but being a mother was an experience that was incomparable. That little baby has now become a poised, gracious, and smart adult. Knowing that I helped to contribute to her success amazes me, and it gives me a huge sense of accomplishment. However, the real justification to my success as a mother comes from my daughter. When I look at the well-versed woman that she has become, I know that I have succeeded in my role as a mother to her. I am by no means perfect, but I am perfect to her. My goal to be a good mother was achieved, and that makes me a success. I have many other strong relationships in my life as well. My relationship with God is foremost, and it has helped me in my relationships with family, friends, and co-workers. I have worked hard at being a good listener and practicing principles of excellence in my interactions with those individuals. Part of my success is having the ability to encourage, motivate, and support others while remaining steadfast and focused on my goals as well.

I know that my success is the result of my hard work, but I have also benefited from the support from others. When I chose my career, I knew that it had to be one that I loved. Teaching children makes me happy. I got my first full-time teaching job twenty-eight years ago when I was still a college student. During my last semester of undergrad, I did a student teaching internship at an elementary school. I remember putting a lot of effort into my appearance when I would show up every day. I wanted to look and act as if I was already employed at the school. I received a lot of positive feedback on my work ethic and professionalism from the teachers and the school principal. I was set to graduate in January of that year, and I desperately wanted a teaching job. I was nearing the end of my internship when the principal of the school approached me about a teaching position. It turned out that one of her teachers was relocating to another city. The principal told me that if I was interested the position, she would set up an interview for me. I was excited beyond measure. For me, it was confirmation that I was doing a good job and making a good impression. I interviewed for the position and I got the job! It was days before Christmas break, and it was such a relief to know that I would have a job at the start of the new year. I began my new job, and I walked into a very overwhelming situation. The previous teacher basically left an insurmountable amount of unfinished work to do. I had little to no time to train prior to starting the job. I didn't feel prepared or confident when I began. But once again, I didn't let those thoughts defeat me. I walked in on the first day resolute to make a positive impact on the lives of children.

Those six months in my new position are now a blur to me. What I do remember is that each day was a new challenge, a fresh learning experience, and a constant struggle. I had feelings of incompetency, frustration, and anxiety, but I didn't allow those feelings to govern me. I used opportunities on my breaks and after school to talk to other successful teachers, and I wasn't afraid to ask questions and learn. Although I had a personal struggle going on inside, I maintained a well-organized class. I made it through the year, and my principal was pleased with my work. More importantly, the children loved me, and they loved learning. In a matter of speaking, we learned together. I had to figure many things out on my own that year, but I relied on my faith in God and my will to succeed to get me through. Those six months laid the foundation for the remaining years of my career that I still love. I carry over these principles in my daily experiences with students in my classroom. I am invested in their success, so I am a leader in my field and in the classroom. Hard work, diligence, and consistency are norms in my professional life, and these norms have helped elevate me toward success.

Some of the strongest feelings of success that are present in all parts of my life have come from my ability to set personal goals for myself. Part of my personal growth over the years has been my ability to push through obstacles to fulfill my life goals. I've celebrated each milestone in my path to success, no matter how big or small it was. Those milestones always put me one step closer to my identified goals. With goal setting, I feel like I am constantly on a journey to do and learn more. Setbacks are seen as such. I don't spend time worrying about what I don't have, rather I reflect on better, more focused ways to achieve what I want. The life that I envision is a possibility in my eyes because I have experienced success in several parts of my life. This motivates me to set higher goals. My competition is with myself to be the best me. Meeting my personal goals has also increased my self-esteem and given me the confidence to search for opportunities that can make me a more marketable professional. I have clarity and focus that make my life happier and remind me that I am truly a success.

God has blessed me with wisdom, determination, and fortitude. I have never run away from a challenge, even when I knew that it may cause unwarranted stress and anxiety. When I specifically think of entrepreneurial success, I imagine that it requires a great deal of sacrifice, hard work, and consistent dedication. I am not an entrepreneur, but I know that my experiences have only driven me to work harder. These principles transfer to life, not just a particular occupation. I have spent my life working and learning, which has made me a more spiritual, educated, and fulfilled woman. My network of personal and professional relationships with friends, co-workers, and associates inspires me to raise the bar. I am now in a position to step out on faith and share my story. Participating in a book anthology definitely was not on my radar, but I am so grateful that I was selected to be a part of this project. While my story may not be particularly unusual, it is real, and it is my story. Whenever I feel inadequate or discouraged, I try not to let those thoughts fester. I focus on things that I know are good in my life, and I use them as incentives to do better. This has been a constant in my daily routine. I hope that my experience will serve as motivation to push forward and celebrate life and what makes you happy. In this context, I am a success. "If we risk nothing, we risk everything." I am willing to take risks to achieve success because for me, my success is my happiness.

Tips for Success:

- ▶ Trust in God. He will provide all that you need and want. With prayer and belief, any and all things are possible.

- ▶ Believe in yourself. You must be your first advocate. If you don't trust that you can achieve success, no one else will. Challenge yourself to step outside your comfort zone. There is always an unexpected opportunity to be great. In the event that there isn't, create one for yourself.

- ▶ Make a list of things that make you happy. Set a plan for how you envision your life and how long it will take for you to get there. Work hard to make your life a success by eliminating negativity and those who don't encourage you to be your best self.

- ▶ Persistence: When obstacles come up that may deter or delay your progress, don't give up. Stay focused on the end goal, and set small milestones along the way until you achieve what you have in mind.

- ▶ Take pride in your life and your accomplishments. You are the director of your life, and only you can direct how you want it to be.

- ▶ Be intentional in your actions and how you interact with others. Live a purposeful life by creating and maintaining meaningful relationships. These are ultimately what matter once you have achieved all of your goals. You'll need positive people around you to share in your success.

The Key Measurement for Success

CHERICIA CURTIS

"'For I know the plans I have for you,' declares the LORD, 'plans to prosper you and not to harm you, plans to give you hope and a future.'"
—Jeremiah 29:11 NIV

Spelling the word "success" is easy. Now here's the tough part. I heard my name over the intercom system loud and clear. "Chericia!" They never did learn to pronounce my name correctly. "You need to come clean up this dog poop out of the kennel, and don't forget the cat kennels are next!" The dog poop wasn't that of a cute little toy terrier, but of a 75-lb lab. You get the picture.

Or what about this one? "Don't forget to go outside and lock up all the cars up." I slowly replied, "But it's 28 degrees outside, and I checked them an hour ago." The sales manager quickly replied, "It doesn't matter. That was an hour ago!"

I remember looking up and whispering to God, "This is not why I went to college!" I thought to myself, "I should be on Broadway somewhere. That's what I went to school for." But I was a 24-year-old single parent, and I knew that I had rent and daycare to pay. My son needed new shoes, and my money was funny. Guess what I did? I got my behind out there, double-checked those locks on the cars, and kept it moving.

That very next day, I sold three cars. I was so happy, but my happiness was short lived. All of the customers wanted full-size spare tires instead of the factory spare tires. I had to lift these 40- to 50-lb tires by myself in three-inch heels while the other sales guys standing on the floor watched me sweat and struggle. Not one of them came out to help me, but that was alright. What doesn't kill you makes you stronger.

Little did I know that all along, God was preparing me for the next level, and the next, and the next. It may not have been the next level I dreamed of, but God *always* knows what's best. So after selling spay and neutering services, Kid n Play House Party Pants, furniture, appliances, electronics, telecommunications, network security, and technology, I realized that the word "success" doesn't come easy and isn't always measured by a W-2 statement. Learning that in itself is a success. There were jobs where I worked 80 hours per week and made half the money I did working 45 to 50 hours per week. But in every situation, God was preparing me for the next step. Keep in mind that a six-figure income can come and go and come back again, but the experience you gain is invaluable. God's plan for you is the truest measure of success.

As I look back on my career, I can confidently say that success is not something that happens overnight; in most cases, it happens over *many* sleepless nights of working tirelessly toward your goals. I do understand one thing: the countless nights of working hard to achieve success mean nothing without a strong faith system and foundation. In Corporate America, there are no wolves in sheep's clothing; there are just wolves. I say this tongue in cheek, but if you don't produce, you'll be reduced. The pressure is nonstop. Just know this going into it and be prepared. In my line of business, you are told "no" many more times than "yes." There are days where the only one who doesn't reject me is Jesus. There have been so many days where my own shadow abandoned me, and all I could do was cry out to God for help. Some days, I just needed to get through the night so I could get up in the morning, only to start the race all over again. Some days, I felt like a hamster on a wheel. Each morning, I gave myself a pep talk: "No pain, no gain, ain't nothing to it but to do it." "The early bird catches the worm, so hit the floor running!" Then there's this one pep talk that I think we as women of color probably said in our mother's wombs: "You're a strong black woman. You *must* bring home the bacon and fry it up in the pan." However, I used the microwave many mornings. I also went through a phase of succumbing to societal pressures. "Chase that dollar, and when you find it, you will have arrived!" But what I soon found out was that no matter what my W-2 statement said, I still had one question. "Okay, now what?"

After 25 years in an industry dominated by white males and pretty much any other ethnicity than mine, I have also learned that man's definition of success may never apply to me. In my humble opinion, I am held to a different standard. I always have been, and I always will be. Being recognized as a successful businesswoman means I have to work harder, sell more, and constantly reinvent myself to prove I even belong in the same room as my white male counterparts. You actually get accustomed to living most of your career under a microscope or heat lamp and in some cases in a mental state of being on the proverbial "hot seat" with no fire extinguisher in sight. Under these conditions, success can get lost in translation and make you begin to doubt yourself and your identity. I had to accept that there would always be someone who told me "you're not good enough." So, I had to learn to let God determine my success, not man. It wasn't easy, but when I did, let me tell you, my life got better. Or rather I should say I finally found peace. I also discovered the answer to the "now what?" Let me explain.

About a decade into my sales career, I got married to a wonderful man who was not only wonderful to me but also a wonderful father to my son. I also was blessed to be a mom to his son who lost his mother to colon cancer before she turned 40. We got married, blended our families, both had careers, and combined our monies to enter the world of the six-figure income. We lived in the suburbs, and the rest is history. Life was good, right? What more could a single mom ask for? A good, God-fearing man to help raise my son and who didn't mind sharing everything he had, including his beautiful child and his paycheck! His benefits weren't bad either. Like I said, the rest was history, but *His* (God's) story for me is what mattered.

Now that I was married and financially stable, I felt I could take chances in my career. For example, I could travel if my job required it because my "boo" was at home if I needed to be out of town overnight. Shortly after getting married and settling into our new home, my former manager, who became one of my closest and dearest friends, called me and told me about a technology company that was hiring for sales reps. She told me that people were making money, and

I mean a lot of money. Mind you, this was during the technology boom, when the internet was the "world wide web." Businesses were buying telecom and networking technology from anyone who was selling it. It was a boom for sure!

I talked to my husband, and of course he said, "Go for it!!" I did, and I got the job. Praise the Lord! I could now take a chance to pursue money with minimal risk. I couldn't have asked for a more perfect scenario.

I was told, now pump the brakes, "Chericia! You can't get the 'choice' accounts. Those are given to those that we know can handle the large commission checks. You have to prove you can handle the small accounts before we give you the 'money-making' account. You're going to get the accounts no one else wants because we know you can handle it." Translation: you will earn every dollar you make. Nothing will come easy, and you will have to compete and fight for every penny you get. Little did I know that God was preparing me for this job years ago, and it started with cleaning poop in kennels. Your path to success will not be like that of others, and oftentimes, you will have to do things others may not have to do.

Once I got started at the new job, I closed some large deals, and God blessed me with some good commission checks. Albeit, I never landed the mega deal that would allow me to retire, nor was I ever able to purchase a Ferrari, but I won't complain. God has been good to me. My sales career was going well, and we were able to live comfortably. I was finally able to purchase my first designer handbag. In spite of the corporate pressures of sales and being a black woman in a white male-dominated industry, in some circles, I could be considered successful. I felt as if I had arrived. I felt great about the job until I lost a major deal. The world of sales is full of ups and downs, rejections, and overcoming objections. Thankfully, I won more than I lost. In spite of my somewhat comfortable lifestyle, something inside of me would always say, "Okay, I achieved this. Now what?"

This is where I answer the question that haunted me for many years, and it wasn't until I intentionally chose to listen to God to discover the answer to my "now what?" question. After moving to the suburbs and life being both manageable and comfortable enough, I still had a void. That success itch was still plaguing me. What was missing? My kids were fine, my husband was great, and I had a little money in savings. I knew that we were blessed, and I was grateful. So, why did I still have this unexplainable void?

One Sunday while at our church, Antioch Christian Fellowship of Corinth, I was enjoying sitting in the congregation and getting my weekly Word from above when I had an interesting experience. Pastor Christopher J Respass preached a sermon that slapped me across my face. "In the end, only what you do for Christ will last," he said. All these years, I'd been looking for success in all the wrong places and all the wrong faces. And if these sound like the lyrics to a song, they are. Just replace the success with love. However, that is also applicable.

My epiphany came to me as clear as day: God's measurement of success is what counts the most. That's when I realized that my career didn't define me, God did. In corporate America, you're only as good as your last sale, but with God, you were good enough when He created you. You see, in His eyes, I was always good enough, no matter what my boss, clients, competitors, or frenemies said. Therefore, any success I have is because of Him. How do I repay Him? Acknowledge that God's success for me is not static, it's dynamic. No matter the job I have, the money I make or don't make, if I am meeting with a CEO, CIO, or CNO (Chief Nobody Officer), I am successful because God says so. With my newfound definition of success, I felt as I could be used by God to do things I never thought I could achieve.

When my definition of success changed, my career began to have more purpose. I knew that no matter what faced me each day in the life of sales, good or bad, God would place me in the position to be successful. For example, I was driving back from Houston after a long day of client meetings when I got a call from my new boss. "Cherikuh, this is [I forgot his name, and as usual, he didn't know how to pronounce mine]. We aren't making our sales numbers as a company, and I am sorry to say we have to let you go." I immediately went into my "Oh no you didn't" spiel. I began to raise my voice just a little. "You mean to tell me I've been growing the business, reviving the dead, building relationships this company has never had, closing deals, and this is how you do me? Oh, I get it. It's because I am a black woman, isn't it? I heard nothing but dial tone after that. I had gotten out of character for a moment and forgot to whom I belonged. I was feeling myself, and my ego was bruised. My success was now in question, and obviously I wasn't good enough, or they wouldn't have let me go. I called my husband, and he said, "Just get home, baby. It's going to be okay." Okay, my foot! They had just let me go, and it had come out of nowhere. All I could think about was what people would think about me when I told them I was let go. I was sure they would think I was a complete failure.

After feeling sorry for myself for a few hours and listening to the Christian radio station, a calm came over me that eased my fears. I heard a voice say, "I determine your success, not man. I knew this was going to happen to you before you left for your trip to Houston. Nothing happens to you that I don't already know about. Now why are you trippin? You're spending all this time ripping and running up and down the road, and I might know what's best for you!" I cried a little bit and whispered, "Okay, God, I trust you." Some weeks later, I continued my job search, and God blessed me with several job offers. That's just how God works when you give it over to Him.

During this time of being in between jobs, I remained heavily involved in the church, and as a matter of fact, I gave even more to Him. I took this time to write plays, sing in the choir, and help with the cancer ministry. I worked for Him like never before and let Him order my steps. I want you to know that when I let God determine my steps, He revealed gifts I never knew I had. I had always dabbled in play writing, but when I prayed that whatever I wrote glorified Him, the clutter became clarity. Not only did God bless me with a new job making more money than I did at the previous job, He blessed me with a successful ministry that would bring people to Christ using my life experiences, my passion, my voice, and my pain as another way to reach people for His purpose.

After writing a few plays and having some level of success, God answered my question yet again. "Now what?"

I continued to measure my success through Him, for Him, and because of Him. I stepped out on faith, and my husband and I started a production company called 2nd Adam Production. Our company develops and creates faith-based stage and screen plays that point all success to Him. He has placed amazing writers, film makers, and executive producers in my path. These wonderful people are extremely gifted, and working with them is nothing short of God led and orchestrated. I had no idea that this was what He had planned for me, and my definition of success had never resembled this. But like I said, my definition of success was always limited and myopic. His definition of success for my life is limitless and eternal.

I now have six stage and screen plays under my belt and many more to come with God's guidance and direction. I am balancing my career, my gift, and my passion only with His help. As I continue to write, produce, direct, and allow Him to dictate my success, if one person is led to Christ, all the success I have had in my career will pale in comparison to the greatest gift we can share with anyone—God's Promise of salvation and eternal life. Don't stress about success. Pray about success. The secret to success is not a secret at all. The Word of God was never intended to be a secret. It was intended to be shared. The thing about God's success for you is that it's for you! You won't have to compromise, cheat, or step on anyone to get it. Remember, there's enough of God's success for everyone. He's just that kind of God. With God, success is not a once-in-a-lifetime event, it's a lifestyle. If you let Him lead you, success will happen, because with Him, we know there is absolutely no failing. Keep dreaming, keep believing, and keep praying! Your road to success may not be a straight line and may have a few detours along the way. After all, what would we need God for if the road to success was easy? Never forget, you have to go through something to get something. As God takes you to higher heights, never stop giving to others.

Key to True Success: God's measurement of success is always best.

A Few Success Nuggets:

- ▶ Don't burn bridges. You never know when you'll have to do a U-turn.
- ▶ Man's measurement of success is fleeting, whereas God's is forever.
- ▶ God is the best CEO for whom you will ever work.

Unscripted Success: An Unordinary and Extraordinary Business Plan

DANA KEARNEY

I closed my eyes and went back to March of 2005 when Village Babies Development Center was birthed. Lee and I had a three-month-old son named Jaelen, who is fondly known as "Jae." I was thankful to God to have a healthy baby. However, I must admit that I was full of bliss when it was confirmed 20 weeks into my pregnancy by an ultrasound that I was having a boy. Our twin girls, Janee and Jade, were 10 years old. I still harbored the feeling of being older than I wanted to be when Jae was conceived. Lee wanted to wait several years before trying to conceive another child. I believed that his decision was based on his trauma from the near-death experience of Jade at three months old. She went in for a routine surgical procedure that led to her going into respiratory and cardiac arrest. She was revived, but she incurred a brain injury, which later resulted in her being diagnosed with cerebral palsy. Lee and I learned that Jade's injury was a result of medical negligence.

As a result of my trauma and lack of trust of others to care for my children, Village Babies Development Center, LLC, or "VBDC," was birthed. Jae was two months old, and I was determined to stay home with him and continue my career as a registered nurse on a part-time basis. No one was going to be left to care for my son after what Jade experienced at the hands of a medical team in which I had entrusted her. I took my trauma and loss of trust in people and used it as an opportunity to use my passion to allow others to trust me with their children. Working as a registered nurse, I had hundreds of lives for which I was responsible, and I embraced the "Practical Nurse Pledge":

"Before God and those assembled here, I solemnly pledge; To adhere to the code of ethics of the nursing profession; To co-operate faithfully with the other members of the nursing team and to carry out faithfully and to the best of my ability."

It was not a business plan that came to mind when VBDC "fell into my lap." A thought crossed my mind to ask my neighbor Karley what her plans were for her son Jack, who was born on Jae's due date of January 3, 2005. She said she had visited some centers, but did not find anything with which she felt comfortable. After explaining my plan, I offered to watch her son, Jack. She and her husband accepted my offer. Lee supported me and posted a flier at a neighboring train station. At first, I was upset with him for posting it, but I realized that this was his way of supporting my interest in watching a few children in our home. As a result of Lee's efforts, I received a call on a Saturday night from a mom named Haley. She stated she was responding to a posting about childcare services. She told me about her son Bradon and her desire to remove him from the current daycare that he was attending. I empathized with her feelings and felt a wave of responsibility. After several days of having Jae, Jason, and Bradon to care for, Claire joined my growing circle of neighborhood children. Claire lived on the block that was parallel to the street I on which lived. I found myself with a total of four children in my care, and it was then that I began to realize that I had to employ someone to assist me.

Lee's first cousin's wife, Marisol, joined me. I had a gut reaction to call Marisol. After all, she was someone I trusted, she was working a per diem job as a teaching assistant, and she would often babysit for family members. Incidentally, Marisol and I spoke about our dreams of starting a business one day. Several years prior to the development of VBDC, we cleaned houses together and would occasionally cook dinners to sell. However, we did not find this to be profitable, and these ideas were short lived. In contrast, after several months of caring for children in my home, we developed a waitlist by word of mouth. Claire's parents, Jen and Erik, were so pleased with our efforts, they gave us an additional $400 a month based on their satisfaction with our services. I asked for a blessing, and I began to realize that I had to learn how to receive what I had asked for. It was an abundant blessing that would grow faster than Marisol and I could manage.

After several months of what I had considered babysitting, I came to realize that this was an actual business. Haley asked me if my house was a licensed family daycare. I remember looking at her and having a sinking feeling. Having to answer "no" felt discouraging to me. However, I took that "no" and turned it into a "yes" by attending a class on registering my home as a family daycare. It was one of many accomplishments for me after beginning my journey into entrepreneurship. In the midst of dealing with my growing pains, I realized that I had to learn the details of receiving revenue. My heart was big, but my knowledge base of business was limited. During the peak of tax filing season, I was asked by several parents for my social security number. I recall feeling angry because I did not realize, until then, that they were reporting payments to the IRS for childcare, which is how business should be respected when paying for a service. I decided that I no longer wanted to give out my social security number. Hence, I reluctantly realized that this was not a babysitting gig. After the growing pains of operating a business began to escalate, Village Babies was incorporated and got a tax ID number. Jen and Erik taught me about the meaning of for-profit versus not-for-profit. My parents began to realize how my business was growing before I realized what was happening. Being involved in the day-to-day operations was beginning to take its toll. My house was no longer my home; it was a business. Lee, Jade, and Janee would come hoping to enjoy full range of the house. However, they became prisoners to their rooms until the children left at 6:30 p.m.

After two years of operating, I obtained an accountant and payroll company. Employees Sasha Morgan and Liza Lashley, who is also a registered nurse, joined VBDC. I began to receive a myriad of requests for child care and was challenged with how to grow this business outside of my house. Jen and Karley offered their homes for me to use for child care as well. I was overwhelmed by God's blessings. At the same time, I was trying to balance this blessing with my family life and growing tensions between Marisol and me. We were working 12-hour days, five days a week. We both had families that we tried to balance with a business demand that grew faster than we could manage. I realized we both had different strengths. My emotions began to shadow my passion as I became frustrated with the fact that I was taking the lead in this fifty-fifty partnership. It was my expectation that the workload and knowledge base would be balanced evenly. I realized that I had to make adjustments and continue to operate with knowing that this business without a plan would fail if my frustrations continued to grow as fast as the blessing that was set upon me.

After three and a half years of operating, Haley's husband, Kris, told me about an existing commercial daycare that was going out of business. His thought was that this building would be the perfect turnkey operation for my growing business. I remember feeling a release of energy in knowing that I could possibly move my business out of my home. I wanted my house back, as I missed sitting in my living room and watching television. Dinner was eaten in our bedrooms because the dining room was the "playroom."

I received an answer to my prayers again after meeting the landlord of the property I would soon be leasing. This commercial building was a prefabricated, three-story, 12,000-square-foot property specifically built to be a child care center with a two-story, one-family house attached to it. During my initial meeting and building tour with Mr. Sachi, I told him I didn't think I could move forward with renting the property. Fear had taken its toll. I looked forward to moving out of my home but I also wondered how I would operate in a commercial setting that could house 100 children. Mr. Sachi looked me in the eye and said, "I have faith and believe that you can do it."

The process of leasing the building through Mr. Sachi was not difficult. However, as an African American woman, the realization of racism and discrimination became a reality for me as I moved up the ladder of success. After overcoming the challenges of new standards that were adopted for opening and operating a childcare center, along with letters to then the Governor of New Jersey about the inconsistencies and resistance I faced when dealing with the red tape for local and state levels, I began to embrace the term "growing thick skin." The many nights of tears and depression began to take a toll on me due to the disproportion between my accounts receivables and accounts payable. Moving from my home to a commercial property led to me using funds from my personal household, Marisol's brother, and a loan from a well-known music artist whose daughter attended my family daycare. For the purpose of anonymity, I will call this famous couple's child Anaya and her parents Claudia and John. It was often difficult to meet payroll. Marisol and I were making less than the employees at times. It was then that I realized what a fifty-fifty partnership meant legally. I recall feeling my weakest when both Sasha and Marisol lost their beloved mothers. It was then that I had to run the business without the people on whom I depended the most to maintain the day-to-day operations.

I believe it was God's grace that kept me above water, and VBDC finally made the move to the commercial building after battling eight months of red tape. There were 25 children enrolled at VBDC on the first day in the new building. The owners of the previous existing child care center would become our biggest challenge. Because their business had changed ownership and names several times and the reputation was not favorable, VBDC had the task of informing potential clients that we had no affiliation with the previous business. The building itself was aesthetically in poor shape. The parents who believed in VBDC rolled up their sleeves and painted the interior of the building, brought furniture for several classrooms, and planted a garden. God's grace and mercy held us together in an effort to maintain my vision to provide a high quality of care for the children within the community.

Viki was the first employee I hired from outside of my home. I was unable to pay her for two months. However, she refused to leave and worked every day to ensure the safety and security of the children. After a year of operating in the new building, there were just under 100 children enrolled at the Center. Marisol and I grew further apart due to our inability to maintain our emotions in the midst of a continually growing business. In the midst of the growing pains, parents assisted us with paperwork and volunteered to help us continue to grow the business.

My personal life began to suffer. My husband and I became strangers. One day, my mother called me to come over to her house. I was uncomfortable with the sound of urgency in her voice. When I arrived, my daughter Janee was sitting on the couch next to me. My mother showed me a copy of a Facebook posting that Janee took a picture of. Lee had been talking with another woman with whom he started an emotional affair. The pain was unreal, and I remember moving to my parents' home. It was hard to take a breath each day as I pondered whether or not my marriage would survive. My relationship with Marisol was in turmoil as well. We were barely speaking. I asked God, "How could a business be doing so well and the 'behind the scenes cast of characters' be falling apart?"

In December of 2011, Marisol and I ended our business relationship, and my director, Star, left shortly thereafter. She was what I refer to as my unsolicited business partner. As I look back, it was only God who held me together. It was one of the lowest parts of my life, yet the business was still thriving. The business continued its growth, and again, I tried to balance the demands. Payroll would go unmet at times, and I continued to use my own personal funds to fund my business.

Fast forward to 2015 when a turn in my life began to take place. After several years of spiritual and marriage counseling with my therapist, Sue, I began to change within myself. It was a process like no other. You see, I learned that I could not control or blame others. I realized that I could only control my own behaviors and actions and that I needed to let go and let God. My health was failing due to uncontrolled high blood pressure, obesity, depression, and anxiety. There were many trips to the emergency room and countless sessions of counseling. Lee and his cousin, Mike, began to grow apart due to the separation of the business partnership between Marisol and me. It was a struggle to watch us come apart within our immediate and extended family.

After several months of self-destruction and declining health, or as Sue called it, being brought to my knees, I lost 40 pounds. My sense of self began to strengthen along with my faith. I was no longer diagnosed with hypertension or long-term depression. My marriage and my relationship with Marisol began to heal. As I became healthier emotionally, I began to disassociate with people who were not true friends. My sincerest friends stayed by my side through it all, and God never left me, although I felt like I was alone at times.

The business grew to an all-time high with an enrollment of 165 children to date. I have a controller of finances and an accountant for my business. While I still endure the challenges that most small businesses face, I learned how to swim effectively with my unscripted plan. One of my favorite quotes says, "You don't always need a plan. Sometimes you just need to breathe, trust, let go and see what happens." — Jean Graziosi

My children have survived the dysfunction of the family during the highs and lows of their mother operating a business and watching their parents work through a marriage that was struggling to survive.

I want all women to understand that success is in the eye of the beholder. You can will what you want and create what you feel with the fear of the Lord and the strength of Goliath. Most often, fear and yourself are your biggest obstacles. You must never give up, no matter how many times you fall or sink below the depths of "hell."

My business is as unscripted as my life, and I am still here to tell my story of a successful business that has survived the brink of disaster from so many angles. It was my faith, my family, and sincere friends that were my support. While the problems and struggle are still present, I see challenges through a different lens now. There is a new group of people that has entered my life, and they bring out the best in me.

When you have a goal, never give anyone the control that would allow them to taint your mind or heart. I have seen many businesses fail because of this. I firmly believe that the best business planner is our Creator. No matter what you call your higher belief system, trust in it with all your heart and soul.

My husband assists me with VBDC. I am happy and grateful that we are approaching our 25th year of marriage. Janee is currently enrolled in a Master's program in Nutrition, Jade is attending college to obtain a certificate in game programming and designing, and Jaelen is in middle school.

VBDC has grown to be a business with a revenue of over $2.5 million and 45 employees. After 12 years of growing my business, it has become my goal to uplift and support my sisters and brothers in their endeavors of becoming entrepreneurs. I have been a mentor and support to several women who are seeking to one day own and operate their own child care center.

In closing, during hard times, I pray and recite the poem by Langston Hughes, *Life Ain't No Crystal Staircase*.

An Equation for Success

DEBORAH RILEY DRAPER

Success is an accomplishment of a goal or aim. This is very personal. It is your goal. It's your aim. Not your mother's or your friend's or your neighbor's or a celebrity friend in your head. Your success is about the attainment of a goal or aim you want to achieve. This has nothing to do with the size, significance, or notoriety of the goal or aim. It has everything to do with you, what you are passionate about, and what delights you so much you want to do the best at it.

Abraham Lincoln said, "Things may come to those who wait, but only the things left by those who hustle." This quote guided me to develop a success equation for myself. This would come in handy as I decided to pursue careers in the advertising and film industries. The default in these industries is the white, male hipster. I am neither a white male nor a hipster, but I am determined to succeed in spite of the fact that these industries are challenging for women and people of color.

I know what it feels like to be treated like an outsider. It doesn't boost your confidence or squarely put success in your sight lines. But the thing about equations is that they don't discriminate. It's input and output. My success equation is easy to apply to any situation. The key is to use it.

Success = Passion + Intent + Discipline + Authentic Self + Preparation. (PIDAP)

This equation was probably born a lot earlier than my passion for these two underrepresented industries. In high school, I took a job at Dairy Queen at the mall. I was fired within the first week for insubordination. I was in the marching band, and Friday nights were the big games. I requested Friday off, and the manager decided to put me on the schedule. I explained that I would be attending the game. He did not remove from me the schedule, and I politely declined the shift. He said, "You are fired." I told my mother. She said, "He did you a favor." My success was not tied to Dairy Queen. The next week, I became the birthday hostess at Chuck E Cheese's.

The interview went like this:

Manager: Do you know what this is?
Me: Yes. Chuck E. Cheese's.
Manager: No. It is an entertainment conglomerate.
Me: Oh.
Manager: Do you know who is the founder of this company?
Me: No.
Manager: Did you even prepare for this interview?
Me: Ummm.
Manager: The founder is Nolan Kay Bushnell. He is also the founder of Atari (and later the technology behind Pixar). He is an innovator. He created the technology for the games in Chuck E. Cheese and the animatronics that make the characters.
Me: That's awesome. I want to work here.

It was a quick interview, but it was a master class. That was my first job in entertainment. I directed the costume characters at the birthday parties and coordinated the on-location appearances. I was a complete success in the role. The factors of the success equations were quietly planted in my head. Everyone has these wonderful seeds already. We must remember to nurture and harvest them.

But as with any of us, you fast forward and life happens. You are working, juggling family, and trying to stay on top of the obligations in your life. You feel so overwhelmed that you can't connect with your authentic self or those wonderful seeds. It's understandable. You feel you have so many others to help (family, co-workers, church family, etc.). Stop. Go back to the equation. Your success will be a blessing, not just to you, but to others as well. However, you have to decide where you are going to put your focus because multi-tasking and focusing on too many things at once yields half-done things.

The first factor in the equation is P, which stands for passion. What drives you and brings you intense excitement when you think about it? Clearly define your passion. This is what sends a chill down your spine in a good way.

Film and television are my passions. I read and watched everything I could about the industry. After college, I landed a job in the advertising business. Yes! I was going to make television commercials. You know the feeling when you are smiling because you feel you are on your way? I was on my way, but not exactly to where I was thinking. I became an executive at an advertising agency after years of hard work, but my passion was to be on the creative side, writing and directing commercials instead of developing the strategy and planning out the campaigns. For years, I wanted to have a lot of involvement with commercials. For example, I wanted to write the copy, be the creative director, and give input on casting and the overall concept. For years, the answer was, "No. You are not on the creative side. You manage the clients." Even if you are told "no," you cannot allow anyone to control or dismiss your passion.

The second factor of the success equation is I, which stands for intent. Train yourself to approach everything with intentionality, especially your passion. Success is not haphazard. Your decision on how to become successful cannot be haphazard either. You are clear about your passion, and you have to apply that same clarity to the decisions you make to bring your passion to life.

Intent and discipline work hand in hand. You have to figure out what to do and do it consistently. No one has to know you are doing it. Find a mentor to help you figure out the steps. In the infancy stage of my scriptwriting pursuits, I did not have a mentor, but I had access to the best writers in the world. You have access to the best in the world, too. I spent time in the library and Barnes & Noble. I introduced myself to the successful writers, and they became my mentors. You don't have to know or even meet all of your mentors. My best lessons came from writers who were gone before I was even born. I purchased books on writing copy and screenplays. I also listened to lectures from prominent writers and copywriters. I wrote the copy for tons of commercials assigned to my agency. No one knew because I did this at home. I was perfecting my craft. I would compare my work to the work presented to the clients. Sometimes my ideas were better, and sometimes they were worse. This exercise was moving me closer to success. When working to accomplish your goals, know that you may only move a few inches at first. Sometimes your progress may not even be visible; just keep moving forward.

Then, it happened. The agency was assigned a big campaign for a major soft drink company. The creative team had two spots approved. An up-and-coming Hollywood director (who would become very famous just a few months later) was selected to shoot the commercials in Los Angeles with a very well-known cast. There were two approved commercials. I had an idea that the campaign should be a trilogy. I went home and created an awesome commercial script. I managed the clients; that was my role, not copywriting. So, I presented my commercial script to the client, not the creative team. She loved it and approved the agency to add the commercial to the campaign and shoot it. The creative team was not so eager about the spot, but the agency president was thrilled to expand the client contract and increase the revenue.

Intentionality is a combination of patience and purpose. You know when it is the right time, and you know when you are ready. Watching that commercial on TV fueled my passion even more. It would be another 10 years before I would see something I wrote on TV again. So, I kept going, getting promoted, and strengthening relationships with clients. I remained passionate, intentional, and disciplined in reading, writing, and researching things about my passion. Eventually, I decided that I would launch my own production company. My mother agreed to help in any way she could; she was even willing to be in a film if I needed her to.

We were so excited about this idea. During this time, my mother was not feeling well, and I took her to the doctor to get some tests done. She was diagnosed with renal cell carcinoma Stage 4. This vibrant woman was given six months to live. I couldn't breathe, and I didn't want to. I couldn't write because my eyes were filled with tears. I called every specialist at every cancer center I knew of. We flew to Cleveland and applied for a special clinical trial, but my mother did not qualify due to her age and how the cancer had spread. The idea of some silly script and fictional characters were so ridiculous because this situation was real. This was life or death. Six months to the day after her diagnosis, my mother died.

I went to visit her grave a few weeks after her death. I drove down the long, windy dirt road to the cemetery. The gate was locked. The tears started to stream down my face. I looked up at the eight-foot gate, and the tears flowed even harder. I sat down on the ground and just couldn't figure out what to do. This trip was a disaster. I had failed. Success at that moment was climbing that fence and getting to the other side. In between the tears, I saw a bug climbing on the fence. I kicked off my pumps and every few minutes unhooked my dress from the chain links as I climbed higher and higher. I reached the top and looked down dizzied from the height and the tears. I closed my eyes, let go, and jumped.

I was in the air for what felt like a very long time, and then I hit the ground. I was dirty but not broken. I succeeded in climbing that enormous fence. I spent the next few hours talking to my mother. I climbed back over the fence and got in the car. Where the dirt road met the paved street was a sign—Coffee Bluff Road. Coffee Bluff Road is where my mother was born, raised, and buried. That day, my production company came to life. Coffee Bluff Pictures was born on Coffee Bluff Road. Every picture I ever direct will pay homage to my mother and the day I jumped.

I discovered what I was made of in this process. So often, I hid and felt uncomfortable standing out. "To thine own *self* be true" became for me more than just a quote from a Shakespeare play. I realized that success would not come to me if I was being who I was supposed to be and letting the world see that person. No apologies. Being good to myself mentally, spiritually, and physically and being good to my goals is authentic. Standing as your authentic self is the only way you will keep standing even when you get knocked down.

Preparation gets you back up when you are knocked down or pulled up. You have to put the work in and be ready for the challenges. Regardless of the career, ambition, or goal, you can't expect to win if you have not prepared for the race. I didn't attend film school, but I read the books, took weekend classes in New York, attended workshops at every film festival I could attend, and volunteered on many sets. Learning is ongoing, and so is preparation. You must be ready every day. Establish your routine every day that gets you prepared not only for what you are expecting to happen, but for what you can't predict. Because if opportunity is knocking, you need to be dressed and ready to go.

My passion was back. The equation proved valid. Success = Passion + Intent + Discipline + Authentic Self + Preparation (PIDAP). These factors propelled me over that eight-foot fence. After that, film and TV would be a piece of cake.

Still, after the jump, I was not writing copy at the ad agency, and my newly formed production company didn't have any assignments. Almost two years to the day after I jumped, I heard a radio broadcast on NPR about a watershed moment in 1973 in Paris that changed the fashion industry forever. Wow. You know when it's your moment. The moment speaks to you. Halston, Bill Blass, Anne Klein, Oscar de la Renta, and Stephen Burrows took on Pierre Cardin, Saint Laurent, Givenchy, Ungaro, and Dior at the Palace of Versailles in an epic matchup for the fashion crown, and the American secret weapon was black models. This was an incredible story, and I knew it would make a great documentary. I gave myself the green light. New York, Paris, beautiful people, beautiful clothes, and an untold story about the contributions of African American women to the fashion industry in the early 1970s was perfect for me. How could I not tell this story? I had passion for the story, and my intent was to direct my first film. I researched the story with intense discipline for three months. I found the people who participated in or witnessed the famed fashion event. After a few unsuccessful email exchanges, I called Stephen Burrows, the legendary fashion designer, on the phone.

Me: Hello, may I speak with Stephen Burrows?
Stephen: Yes. This is he.
Me: This is Deborah Riley Draper. I'm the film maker who is writing and directing the project about the Versailles fashion show of 1973. I will be in New York in two weeks and want to interview you for the film.

Stephen: Oh, right. I didn't know you had started production. Let me check my calendar and get
back to you.

My authentic self showed up on that call. It was the first time
I said out loud that I was a film maker. I nailed an interview
with the only black designer to participate in the legendary
Grand Divertissement at Versailles show. I had my first shoot
for my first film scheduled. Now, I only needed a crew and a
ticket to New York.

You can't be afraid to ask for what you want. Your
authentic self knows just what to do when all of the other
factors are already in place. I was prepared, and using
my connections I had made volunteering on a film festival
committee, I secured the director of photography (DP) from
The Walking Dead to be my DP on the shoot. After securing
him for my film, he pulled together the rest of the crew from
his Rolodex. He would become the DP for the entire film
and my second film, too. Your success will bring success and
opportunity to the others around you, and that collaboration
fuels your discipline and preparation.

The process was not easy, but the success equation
guided me. All the factors would support me in writing,
directing, and producing a film. You can't waiver on your
passion. Eighteen months later, I had a finished film with
shoots in New York, Paris, and the famed Château de Versailles. Now what?

The thing about success is that success is not finite.
Every success begets the start of another quest to success—
and another set of obstacles, thus, a new set of variables in the

equation. The good news is that the formula does not change, and success builds upon success. This does not mean there won't be missteps, miscues, and missed opportunities. There will be. The discipline keeps you focused and determined.

With a finished film in hand, the next step would be to get it released. I wanted it in theatres, on TV, and video on demand (VOD). I didn't know anyone in distribution. I didn't have an agent or representation. My research and all of pop culture pointed me to the Cannes Film Festival. I planned to submit the film to Cannes. The feedback from a few in my circle was not encouraging. They said that the Cannes Film Festival was for the major players and the really good films. They told me that having my film featured was a long shot. They said, "Don't get your hopes up. You probably won't get in."

When someone on your side tries to dim your light, you feel hurt and upset about it. However, I submitted anyway. Anger and doubt are never part of the equation. They get in the way of the real factors. Passion + Intent + Discipline + Authentic Self + Preparation = Success. There is no room in the equation for negative energy. Your authentic self is the A-list version of you, not the second-rate version that someone else projects on to you. Seeking the approval of others should not be confused with seeking advice or guidance. Advice or guidance is about what steps to take, not about who you are. Shakespeare very clearly gave the best advice about how to handle the haters: "To thine own self be true." It was sound advice in 1609 and is sound advice now.

In my case, the naysayers were right. I didn't get in the festival as an Official Selection, but I got in. I received a market screening. My film would play on May 12, 2012, at

5:30 p.m. in the Palais J screening room. My film was listed in the screening schedule with the major studios and independent films from around the world.

At 5:28 p.m., no one was in my screening except four members of my crew who traveled to Cannes to support me. I was there in a screening room at the Cannes Film Festival, holding the screening with the same vigor for my four crew members as if it were for 444 people. But right before the lights went down, a flood of people rushed in. The film screened to an audience that included the *Hollywood Reporter, Women's Wear Daily*, a couple of Hollywood producers, and international buyers. An L.A.-based producer asked me to meet him the next morning for breakfast at the Carlton Hotel. I was taking my first meeting to discuss distribution. I was ready and well prepared. That meeting led to *Versailles '73: American Runway Revolution* receiving an option from a big-name Hollywood director, who optioned the documentary to turn it into a big-budget movie. The narrative feature of my documentary is now in development, and I will serve as an executive producer.

That screening propelled the film to open Fashion Week in New York and Toronto. It became an official selection in over 20 festivals around the world. It was at a theatrical release in L.A., and an acquisitions buyer from Viacom saw it. She offered a deal to bring the broadcast premiere to a Viacom Network. Ten years after that first commercial I wrote, I sat at home and watched the broadcast premiere of my first film on television.

Success = Passion + Intent + Discipline + Authentic Self + Preparation. This equation schooled me and guided me in producing not just one film, but writing, directing, and producing a second film, *Olympic Pride, American Prejudice*, which garnered an NAACP Image Award nomination in 2017. Now, Coffee Bluff Pictures has projects in development. I still work as an advertising agency executive, but now, the creative teams can't put me in a box and dismiss my creative input or feedback. My creative credentials can stand toe-to-toe with anyone else's in the building. That is success for me.

The beauty of the success equation is its honesty and transparency. It can be applied to all situations where you need to move the cursor from where you are to where you want to be. You have to show up and put in the work to solve the equation. It's doable.

Passion: Define what makes you excited and feeds your soul.

Intent: Be very clear about your purpose. Take deliberate actions and remove the people, places, and things that create chaos. Intentionality is never indiscriminate.

Discipline: Do the work. Do the work today, tomorrow, and the day after. Establish the rules of how you are going to conduct yourself on this path.

Authentic Self: Remember Shakespeare's timeless words of wisdom: "To thine own self be true."

Preparation: You have to be ready when the opportunity comes, when the phone rings, when the email arrives. Preparation doesn't delay or procrastinate.

Put this together, and you will achieve success. And remember, success is not measured by standards set by anyone other than you. No two successes look alike or have the same timetable. My success took many years to attain, and there will be many more years of working this equation to achieve greater success.

Success is as honest as math. You put in a variable and add another, and the sum of the whole will be greater than the parts. So solve for the Xs in your equation and don't leave anything blank. Your success depends on it.

ABOUT THE AUTHORS

Becky A. Davis

Chief BOSSpreneur® Becky A. Davis is known as the "Entrepreneur's Secret Weapon" for her straightforward coaching skills that develop individuals into well-rounded business owners. Becky works as a Business Growth Architect with a construction crew of experts who design business growth blueprints to help clients build their dream business. She is a member of Forbes Magazine Coaches Council and is the official entrepreneur coach for the ultra-exclusive Odyssey Media Company, executive coach for Black Enterprise Women of Power Summit, and national entrepreneur spokesperson for The Coca-Cola Company's women small business initiative. Becky is one of the most in-demand experts for small businesses and leadership.

Becky has been featured in media including ABC, FOX, *Forbes, Essence, Black Enterprise, Associated Press*, and *Huffington Post*. She is a sought-after speaker and the author of seven books. Learn more at www.beckyadavis.com and follow her @bosspreneur.

Sherrell Valdezloqui

A media expert with seven years of experience as a magazine publisher, a licensed and ordained evangelist, an entrepreneur, and a U.S. Army veteran, Sherrell Valdezloqui has shown that she's passionate about helping others pursue their purpose. Her dedication lends itself to her abilities to attract over 55,000 followers via social media. As a wife and mother of three, she understands what hard work means and has been recognized for her devotion to and understanding of business, ministry, and social media. Today, she continues to look for new ways to spread her message of hope, fortitude, and positivity to men, women, and children around the world.

Contact Sherrell at todayspurposewoman@gmail.com

Leah Frazier

Leah Frazier is a leading FashionPreneur™. She was recognized in 2015 as one of the most successful women in Dallas and was recently awarded as Fashion Group International's "Rising Star" in Fashion Blogging for 2017. She is an award-winning journalist, certified personal shopper, media personality, radio host, Professor of Marketing, and attorney. She is now Editor in Chief of *Inspire N Style Magazine.*

Leah has been featured on Vogue.com, Examiner.com, CBS Local, Fox TV, CW33, NBC, Good Morning Texas, *Haute Living Magazine, DFW Style Daily*, and many other outlets. She has also cultivated partnerships with Belk, Cantu Beauty, Marshall's, Vogue, Brahmin, Neiman Marcus, Warner Bros., and more.

Recently, Leah expanded her brand to create Think Three Media, a full-service agency offering content marketing, social media marketing, and public relations services for small businesses, entrepreneurs, local artists, and non-profit organizations. Leah can be contacted at LeahFrazier.com

Courtney Williamson

Courtney Williamson is a student-athlete leader with a heart to serve. Over the course of her high school career, she has participated in cheerleading, track and field, and soccer. She won the 2016 TAPPS 5A Soccer Championship. Courtney has been a member of the student government for the last two years and has served in various leadership academies that awarded her the opportunity to travel internationally.

As an active leader and student, Courtney is being sought after by many colleges and universities. In the fall of 2018, Courtney plans to attend college as a pre-med student. Her dream is to become a pediatrician who provides a better quality of life for children around the world.

Courtney is the daughter of Russell and Cheryl Williamson. She resides in Texas with her brother, Russ Jr., and sister, Lauren.

For more information, please visit her blog,
onedayiwillbeblog.wordpress.com

Pearl Chiarenza

Pearl Chiarenza has been the owner of Bodyworks Health & Wellness Center for the past six years. Her clients collectively have lost over 8,000 pounds. In 2009, she herself lost 57 pounds and has maintained her weight loss. Pearl understands that to give fully to others, we must first take care of ourselves. It is one of the reasons she founded her company in 2011.

She also founded Women's Successful Living, hosting events that include coaching women to put themselves first by setting goals for their personal lives, allowing them to properly take care of their families and achieve their dreams. She personally balances her business and family life so that she can also give to back to her community with much grace and finesse.

In 2016, her company was voted "Best of Brandon" and "Best of Southshore" in the Tampa metro area.

Learn more by visiting us at BodyworksHWC.com

Lynn Brockman

UGLYDollFace was founded by Lynn Brockman in 2015. She has over 15 years of experience in the world of luxury fashion and event planning. Lynn Brockman was most recently the Regional Manager overseeing the U.S. accounts for LXRandCo, General Manager at Barney's New York, an Executive at Saks Fifth Avenue, and South East Regional Manager for MaxMara. During her time in these various roles, she advised buyers from Neiman Marcus, Saks Fifth Avenue, Nordstrom, Bloomingdales, Macy's, and Barneys New York, just to name a few. She was also responsible for planning and executing elevated events in these positions.

Lynn is always asked, "Why did you name your company UGLYDollFace?" Her response is always the same: "UGLY-DollFace is about transformation of a person, place, or thing. UGLYDollFace is finding beauty in everything. UGLYDoll-Face is me and it's you. U.G.L.Y = U Gotta Love Yourself!"

Nancy Fuller Garland

Art is a part of Nancy's soul. Her passion for design and "all things beautiful" blossomed when she was in her late 20s. The Fort Worth designer did not discover her passion for jewelry until years later.

Nancy has launched herself to designer status and creates jewelry that commands attention from an adoring and loyal following of clients. "I can see something, a color or art form, and I think to myself, I can translate that into a piece of jewelry. If I love it, I believe other women will as well—we all cherish beauty."

Nancy has been featured in several magazines. Her creations can be found in some of the top boutiques throughout the Dallas area. She spends countless hours in her home studio making jewelry that can accessorize any outfit.

She is a wife, a mother, and a proud member of Delta Sigma Theta Sorority.

Kameron Jones-Marzette

Kameron Jones-Marzette is an educator from St. Louis, Missouri. She has over 28 years of experience in the classroom. She has spent her life pouring into the lives of children by providing a nurturing yet challenging learning environment. She promotes 21st-century skills, and her goal is to motivate children to become lifelong learners and global thinkers. Kameron is a strong proponent of education, women's empowerment, and community service. She has a diverse educational background with degrees in Elementary and Special Education, Educational Leadership, and Adult and Higher Education. She is currently completing a degree in Library and Information Sciences as she begins to transition into new career opportunities in the educational field.

Kameron is the mother of one daughter, Katelyn, and she has been married for twenty-four years to Terry Marzette Jr.

Connect with Kameron at knjomarzette@gmail.com

Chericia Curtis

Chericia Curtis is a sales rep for one of the world's Top 10 Global Technology companies. She has been in the technology industry for over 20 years, and she has held various sales roles. She is also CEO of 2nd Adam Productions, a faith-based production company that focuses on positive and motivating family-oriented content and visual media. Her current projects include Soul Purpose, Old Christmas Tree, and Soul Encounters. She is also executive producer for the upcoming sitcom, The Perfect Family.

She devotes her spare time to her husband and sons and has lived in the city of Highland Village, Texas for over 18 years. She is very active in her church, Antioch Christian Fellowship, in Corinth, Texas, under the leadership of Pastor Christopher J. Respass. She is also a member of the Alpha Kappa Alpha Sorority, Incorporated. She enjoys writing, exercising, cooking, and spending time with family and friends.

Dana Kearney

Dana is the proud daughter of Ronald and Emma LeGrand and the sibling to a twin brother Daryl and younger sister Dori. Her parents have been married for 50 years, and she is blessed to have become a part of their union.

Lee is Dana's husband of almost 25 years, and they have three blessings named Janee, Jade, and Jaelen. They currently reside in South Orange, NJ.

Dana's career started in nursing, as she had been a registered nurse for 15 years prior to becoming the successful business owner of Village Babies Development Center, LLC or "VBDC." VBDC has cared for and educated children between the ages of zero and five years of age for the last 12 years. She also mentors future entrepreneurs in the community.

Dana gives thanks to God and her family and friends who have supported her without fail.

Get in touch with Dana at danakearney3@gmail.com

Deborah Riley Draper

Deborah Riley Draper is a compelling filmmaker and advertising agency veteran, currently serving as the Group Executive Director at Ogilvy. A 2016 Film Independent Lab Fellow, Draper was named to the "2016 Top 10 Documakers to Watch" list for Variety Magazine. Her film work includes the documentary Olympic Pride, American Prejudice, a 2017 nominee for the NAACP Image Awards Outstanding Documentary–Film and qualifier for the 2017 Oscars race; the film's theme song, "Find My Victory"; and her debut film, Versailles '73: American Runway Revolution. She is currently working on two additional features with Wyolah Films.

Draper's leadership in advertising can be seen in major campaigns and projects for Lamborghini, Coca-Cola, Exxon-Mobil, HP, AT&T, and Holiday Inn Express. She has earned two regional Emmys, a Gold Effie, and several Addy Awards.

Draper, a die-hard FSU Seminole, resides in Atlanta and is a member of Film Fatales Atlanta.

Cheryl Polote-Williamson

Nationally acclaimed bestselling author, transformational speaker, and success coach Cheryl Polote-Williamson has established multiple platforms, dedicating her consulting practice to cultivate innovative business solutions, strategic marketing initiatives, and financial acumen for entrepreneurs. A global leader, Cheryl is the CEO and founder of Williamson Media Group, LLC, and Cheryl Polote-Williamson, LLC, where her knowledge and expertise are used as a conduit to affirm others in pursuit of their purpose.

Cheryl's unmatched credibility in the industry has earned her numerous awards, including the Chocolate Social Award for best online community, the Dallas Top 25 Award, and the Female Success Factor Award. She has been named amongst the Who's Who In Black Dallas Publishing, held a position on the Forbes Coaches Council, and participates in the NAACP Author Pavilion, the Congressional Black Caucus, Christian Women in Media, and the National Association of Women Business Owners.

A prolific author and winner of the 2017 Indie Author Legacy Awards, Cheryl has published multiple books, including *Soul Reborn, Words From the Spirit For The Spirit,*

Safe House, Affirmed, Soul Talk, Soul Bearer, and *Soul Source,* with more titles on the way. She is also producing a play entitled Soul Purpose, set for a 2018 debut.

Cheryl and her husband, Russell, currently reside in Flower Mound, Texas. They have three beautiful children, Russell Jr., Lauren, and Courtney, as well as an adorable granddaughter, Leah. In her spare time, Cheryl enjoys traveling, reading, serving others, and spending quality time with family and friends.

To learn more, visit her website at
www.cherylpwilliamson.com

CREATING DISTINCTIVE BOOKS
WITH INTENTIONAL RESULTS

We're a collaborative group of creative masterminds
with a mission to produce high-quality books to position
you for monumental success in the marketplace.

Our professional team of writers, editors, designers,
and marketing strategists work closely together to ensure
that every detail of your book is a clear representation
of the message in your writing.

Want to know more?
Write to us at info@publishyourgift.com
or call (888) 949-6228

Discover great books, exclusive offers, and more at
www.PublishYourGift.com

Connect with us on social media

@publishyourgift

CPSIA information can be obtained
at www.ICGtesting.com
Printed in the USA
FFHW012112261018
48991301-53254FF